ICE

for less

GW00367735

the guidebook that pays for itself in one day

The *for less* Guidebook series...

- 288-page guidebooks
- Detailed fold-out street maps
- Discount card that gives up to 4 people great savings at 300 of the city's best places (*attractions, museums, restaurants, shops, tours etc*).

The *for less* Compact Guide series...

- 76-page guidebooks
- Detailed fold-out street maps
- 2-for-1 (or 50%) discounts at top attractions and museums

...PLUS 50 more *for less* Compact Guides to follow

www.for-less.com

Iceland
for less

Compact
Guide

Publisher Information

First published in Great Britain in 2000 by Metropolis International (UK) Ltd.

ISBN 1 901811 24 7

COPYRIGHT

DISCLAIMER

Assessments of attractions, hotels, museums and so forth are based on the author's impressions and therefore contain an element of subjective opinion that may not reflect the opinion of the publishers.

The contents of this publication are believed to be correct at the time of printing. However, details such as opening times will change over time. We would advise you to call ahead to confirm important information.

All organizations offering discounts in this guidebook have a contract with the publisher to give genuine discounts to holders of valid *for less* vouchers.

The publisher and/or its agents will not be responsible if any establishment breaches its contract (although it will attempt to secure compliance) or if any establishment changes ownership and the new owners refuse to honour the contract.

Care has been taken to ensure that discounts are only offered at reputable establishments, however, the publisher and/or its agents cannot accept responsibility for the quality of merchandise or service provided, nor for errors or inaccuracies in this guidebook.

The publisher will not be held responsible for any loss, damage, injury, expense or inconvenience sustained by any person, howsoever caused, as a result of information or advice contained in this guide except insofar as the law prevents the exclusion of such liability.

PUBLISHER

Metropolis International
222 Kensal Road
London W10 5BN
England

Tel:
+44-(0)20-8964-4242

Fax:
+44-(0)20-8964-4141

E-mail:
admin@for-less.com

Web site:
www.for-less.com

US Office:
Tel:
+1-(212)-587-0287

Fax:
+1-(212)-587-0247

ABBREVIATIONS

☎   Telephone Number
🕐   Opening times

Contents

HOW TO OBTAIN DISCOUNTS

Many of the museums and attractions n this guide offer discounts to holders of this book.

Museums and attractions which offer a discount are highlighted in pink in the ext and designated by the following symbol in the margins:

To obtain your discount, simply hand in he appropriate voucher from the back of his book when you purchase your ticket.

Introduction to Iceland

Iceland's 270,000 inhabitants are bound together by a strong sense of national heritage that causes them to identify unreservedly with their country and with each other. Unlike less isolated cultures, Icelanders are shaped by their landscape, their climate and their history.

This formative environment of ice and fire is suitably dramatic. Its location just south of the **Arctic Circle** means that between May and early August it is never truly dark and Icelanders willingly embrace a period of summer hyperactivity. By comparison, winters are long and grey, with only a few short hours of twilight to interrupt the seemingly endless darkness of the night.

The main attraction for visitors is without doubt the breathtaking North Atlantic scenery. The landscape is rugged, sometimes eerily so, with a mass of craters, mountains, glaciers, geysers, hot springs, ice caps and waterfalls. It is all too easy to understand why in the 1960s NASA chose **Mount Askja** as a practice ground for landings on the moon.

Rivers of ice have hammered valleys and chiselled sharp mountain ridges, and where these glaciers meet the sea, icebergs result. Contrary to widely held preconceptions, Iceland's glaciers and ice caps were not formed in the **Great Ice Age** three million years ago, but in a cool

Reflections

"Iceland is not a myth; it is a solid portion of the earth's surface" – Pliny Miles

Fields of ice

eriod around 500 BC. Today only 10% of
s 103,000sq km (40,000sq miles) is still
overed in ice.

eologically, Iceland is an unruly teenager.
ne of the youngest land masses in the
orld, unsettled and fractious, it is a
haracter in formation, changing and
aturing under the watchful eyes of
eologists the world over.

he source of its youthful ill-temper is the
3,000km (11,000-mile) **Mid-Atlantic
idge**, which dissects the island from
outhwest to northeast. Here, where the
rican and **American** plates diverge at the
arming rate of 2cm (0.8in) a year, the
cenery is marked by volcanic craters, hot
orings and earthquakes. While the
orthwest and east of the country are now
afe" zones, the rest of the island
emains under the menacing shadow of
uptions and earthquakes.

eland is one of the most volcanically active
eas in the world, and it has been
timated that a third of all the lava to have
rfaced in the last millennium has done so
ere. Eruptions from volcanoes above
ound are not the only threat. Subglacial
uptions deep below the surface of an ice
p have given rise to the table mountains
Búrfell and **Bláfjall** at **Lake Mývatn** (page
7). In 1963, the islet of **Surtsey** (page 26)
as born of an ocean-floor eruption, and
n years later, the nearby island of **Heimaey**
as all but lost to a torrent of lava from a
bglacial volcano (page 25).

ith characteristic resilience and
etermination, Icelanders have learnt to
pe with – and to some degree harness
their volatile environment. Geothermal
ergy provides 85% of Iceland's heating
d feeds the open-air recreational pools
central to Icelandic culture, as well as
oviding for the greenhouses where
cessary vegetables are grown. Since
904, hydroelectric power stations have
awn on Iceland's glacial rivers to cover
e needs of the population as well as
dustrial plants.

ore important to the Icelandic economy
an geothermal power, however, is the
hing industry, which by some estimates

Reflections

"There vast and
boundless fires are to be
found, phenomenal frosts
and glaciers, boiling
springs and violent ice-
cold streams" – from the
King's Mirror, written 700
years ago

Catch of the day

Reflections

"The map of Iceland has been sometimes drawn by schoolboys as an eider duck, quacking with wide-opened beak"
– Collingwood

accounts for over 70% of total GNP (gross national product). Hardly surprising, then, was the level of patriotic passion aroused during the **Cod Wars** with the UK, when the fishing boundaries were repeatedly fixed and overturned from 1959 until the dispute was finally resolved with fishing limits set at 322km (200 miles) in 1976.

A further 2% of the GNP stems from agricultural exports, namely lamb, wool and dairy products. Crop growing is not widespread, partly because the climate is too harsh and partly because of the problems of soil erosion.

According to Ari the Learned's 12th-century *Landnámabók* (Book of Settlement), when Iceland was first settled in the late 9th century it was covered in trees "from the mountains to the sea", although this could be a reference to dwarf birch, willow or merely scrub. Extensive use of wood for fuel and mismanaged grazing account for today's lack of trees, although planting initiatives are now set to change the face of Iceland.

In such an environment, it is to be expected that the population may exhibit signs of eccentricity. Icelanders can appear aloof to strangers (certainly their society has been little diluted by foreign blood), but like their land, beneath this cool exterior lies an unparalleled warmth.

In June and July, the ingrained Protestant work ethic gives way to partying and Icelanders take to the roads of their beloved country in their droves after the ten impassable winter months.

Icelanders certainly more than
compensate for any summer laxness
during the rest of the year, when the
working week – often between 50 and 80
hours – is the longest in Europe. It is not
hard to see why. Alongside the high
standards of living and low unemployment
is the dour reality that life in Iceland is
expensive. Imported items cost up to four
times the price in their country of origin.

Despite the cost of such items and the
strong rural tradition, Iceland is without
doubt a consumer society. Possessing the
latest gadgets is of paramount importance.
Icelanders support three daily newspapers,
six TV channels and dozens of radio
stations, as well as drinking more soft
drinks and using more mobile phones per
head of population than most of their
European neighbours. It is nevertheless
largely a classless society.

Irrespective of age or profession,
Icelanders at rest either relax in a
geothermal pool or
enjoy the
wholesome air and
rich landscape,
whether on foot,
horseback or snow
scooter. Whatever
the season, visitors
can also make the
most of these
traditional Icelandic
pursuits. Most
come in the
summer, and
between mid-
September and
mid-May many
museums, hotels
and transport links
close. This should
not deter winter
tourists, however,
who will experience
the *real* Iceland,
complete with snow
and ice and
without the
summer crowds.

Reflections

"Alone in Iceland you are
alone indeed and the
homeless, undisturbed
wilderness gives
something of its awful
calm to the spirit. It was
like listening to noble
music, yet perplexed and
difficult to follow" – Miss
Oswald

IF YOU DO ONE THING . . .

1. If you visit one museum . . .
the **Árbærsafn** (page 17)

2. If you visit one church . . .
Hallgrímskirkja (page 15)

3. If you visit one sculpture gallery
. . . **Ásmundarsafn** (page 17)

4. If you do one trek . . .
Reykjavegur trail (page 18)

5. If you go to one nightclub . . .
Gaukur á Stöng (page 54)

6. If you visit one island . . .
Heimaey (page 25)

7. If you go to one open-air museum
. . **Byggðasafn Skagfirðinga** (page 41)

8. If you go on one shopping spree
. . . **Kringlan** (page 51)

9. If you go on one tour . . .
Golden Circle (page 56)

10. If you do one activity . . .
horse riding (page 56)

History of Iceland

The Icelandic tendency to relate with pride events of bygone eras – what the scholar Sigurður Norðal wryly described a "cashing cheques on deeds committed 700 years ago" – may stem from a defensive need to confound beliefs held by the outside world that Iceland is a small and insubstantial island on the margins of Europe.

The first settlers were **Irish monks** at the end of the 8th century. About a century later, the **Norwegian Vikings** arrived in plundering hordes. The 12th-century *Íslendingabók* (Book of Icelanders) name the first intentional settler as **Ingólfur Arnarson** (page 12), the man who founde **Reykjavík**.

At about the same time, **Flóki Vilgerðarsc** was exploring the island. According to th *Landnámabók* (Book of Settlement), which gives details about the period of intense colonization between 874 and 930, Flóki gave Iceland its name after seeing "a fjord full of drift-ice" in the northwest.

Iceland lays claim to perhaps the oldest democratic institution in existence. In the 10th century each community established a *Þing*, which reported to a general assembly, the *Alþing*, then based at inlan **Þingvellir**.

From 930 to 1030 the *Alþing* gathered once a year to wield legislative and judicia power. However, upholding the peace between sparring chieftains was impossibl because it did not also exercise executive power. This period is remembered for its bloody feuds, many of which were made i defence of a man's honour or from family loyalty.

At the *Alþing* in 1000, Iceland was declared a **Christian** nation. Religion, spread by missionaries, was used as a too to increase Norwegian power on the island. **Bishoprics** were founded and a fe families dominated local politics under th control of the Norwegian king, **Olaf Tryggvason**.

Against this backdrop of change from a

Reflections

"Land, nation and language – the only true trinity" – the poet Snorri Hjartason

eathen to a Christian society, the lives of
ne early settlers, social and political
vents, myths, legends and romantic
nterludes, were all recorded in Iceland's
reat **sagas**.

ney paint a picture of the bloody yet
eroic golden age of Viking morality, where
is "better to die honourably than live on
n shame", as is succinctly recorded in the
Vóamanna Saga. Despite the time lag
etween the events described and the time
f writing, the sagas have until recently
een accorded the status of historical fact,
roviding us with much of our
nderstanding of North European history
uring this period. Revisionist academics,
owever, have dismissed them as little more
nan appealing works of fiction.

ne reverence evoked by the sagas reveals
uch about the Icelandic character. Their
lace in the national consciousness stands
rm. Until recently, there was no television
n Thursday nights and even now on
hristmas Eve the television stops
roadcasting between 4pm and 9pm in an
ttempt to sustain the tradition of
Jöldvaka, when families retold the sagas
round the hearth.

ne identity of those who recorded the
agas is not known, although the chieftain
norri Sturluson is accepted as one of the
ost important. Amongst his works is the
iga about the likeable warrior **Egill
kallagrímsson**. This Viking was himself of
literary bent, being the chief protagonist
f *skaldic* poetry. The story goes that Egill's
oetic prowess saved his life when the
öfuðlausn ("head ransom") poem he

Reflections

"The tourist sights have
nothing like Stonehenge,
The literature is all about
revenge.
And yet I like it if only
because this nation
Enjoys a scarcity of
population"– W. H. Auden
in *Letters from Iceland*
(1936)

þingvellirhses

penned before his execution flattered his gaoler monarch into freeing him.

One of the most famous sagas of all is the *Njáls Saga*, in which the doings of the hero **Njáll** are recounted. Another is the *Vinland Sagas*, which records the exploits of **Leif Eiríksson** (son of another saga hero **Eirík the Red**), whom Icelanders maintain

In the east, Snaefellsjokull glacier presides over an area rich in saga associations

discovered North America 500 years before Columbus.

The *Sturlunga Saga* records the feuds and power struggles of the disruptive **Sturling Age**, which facilitated the increase in Norwegian power. In 1262 this culminated in the Norwegian king **Hákon** being invited to take control to avert internal chaos.

In 1387 the **Act of Union** united Norway (including Iceland as one of its provinces) Sweden and Denmark under Danish rule. Clashes between church and state followed, and in 1550 the Danish government implemented the **Reformation**. The last troublesome Catholic bishop, Jón Arason of Hólar, was beheaded and much of the church's power and possessions passed to the monarchy.

Did You Know...?

The level of literacy in Iceland is 100% and more books are published here per capita than in any other country in the world.

The Danish monarchy also established a trade monopoly, which meant that from 1602 until its annulment in 1787 Icelanders had no choice but to buy poor quality goods from Danish and Swedish firms.

Extensive surveys of Iceland in 1752 led limited modernizations. A postal service

as introduced and small industries were
ncouraged. Improvements were dogged
y a series of natural catastrophes,
owever, and finally halted in 1783 when
he **Laki** volcano erupted. Its poisonous
ava plunged the country into starvation
nd decline.

n 1800 the Danish king discontinued the
Alþing. The ripples of change arrived in
he form of the **Napoleonic Wars**, which
pread revolutionary attitudes throughout
urope and prompted the Danish king to
nnounce extensive reforms. With the
issemination of **Jón Sigurðsson**'s (page
3) patriotic ideas, the struggle for
ndependence was well under way.

n 1845 the *Alþing* was reintroduced, in
855 free trade was reintroduced, in
874 Iceland was granted its own
onstitution, and by 1904 it was enjoying
ome rule. Improvements were made in
ducation, transport and industry, and the
pside of trade disruption in the **First
World War** was greater independence from
enmark. In 1918 Iceland assumed the
tatus of an independent state within the
kingdom of Denmark.

he effect of the **Second World War** was
ikewise perversely beneficial as Iceland's
solation was breached. When Denmark
ell to the Nazis in 1940 Iceland was
ccupied by the British for protection.
British spending and improvements to the
ountry's infrastructure spelt renewed
rosperity. In a stronger position than ever
efore, Iceland argued that its ties with
enmark were no longer valid. Full
ndependence was finally declared on 17
une 1944, Jón Sigurðsson's birthday.

merican troops had replaced the **British**
n 1941. They still maintain a naval base
t **Keflavík** in return for defending
celand. Initial dissatisfaction in the face
f continued foreign presence after the
econd World War has given way to
cceptance of the revenue 4,000
mericans represent. Today, Iceland is a
member of the **United Nations** and **NATO**,
nd its role as a fully fledged member of
he international community was
onfirmed when in 1986 **Reagan** and
orbachev met at the **Höfði** (page 16).

Reflections

Perhaps the best-known
contemporary writer is
Halldór Laxness, who was
awarded the Nobel Prize
for Literature in 1995. His
most important work is
Sjalfstættfolk
(Independent People), not
least for its refusal to
subscribe to the tradition
of romanticizing the
everyday difficulties
faced by Icelandic
peasants.

Reykjavík

The smallest and northernmost capital in Europe is derided by some as little more than an oversized village. Certainly, the atmosphere is arguably the most relaxed and approachable of any European capital. The relaxed village-like feel belies a city that is in fact the country's undisputed political and business centre. It is here that nearly two-fifths of the entire country live and work, and culturall no other Icelandic town can compete with its range of entertainments.

Alþinghúsið

Austurvöllur
🕐 Closed to the public.

The Tjörn beneath a carpet of snow

Reykjavík was the first place in Iceland to be intentionally settled. Story has it that the Norwegian Viking **Ingólfur Arnarson**, i accordance with respected tradition, hurled the pillars of his high seat – symbc of his homestead – into the sea and vowe to the pagan gods to live wherever they came ashore. Three years later, around AI 870, the slaves of the Vikings found them and Ingólfur arrived.

Dómkirkjan

Austurvöllur
☎ 551 2113
🕐 Mon-Sat: 9am-5pm.
Sun: open for services.

When Ingólfur first saw his new home, he named it Reykjavík, which means "Smoky Bay", and refers to the steam he saw rising from the geothermal springs in today's **Laugardalur** area. Ironically, the city is now popularly known as the "smokeless city", in recognition of its wonderful pollution-free atmosphere.

Ingólfur built his farm between the **Tjörn** (the lake) and the sea, growing crops at **Austurvöllur**, the present town square. Th statue there is of Jón Sigurðsson, the popular nationalist who first campaigned for independence in the mid-19th century. When it was finally achieved in 1944, 17 June was chosen as the official date because it was his birthday.

Overlooking the square is an imposing grey basalt building, the **Alþingshúsið** constructed in 1881 to house the *Alþing* (Parliament) that moved here from Þingvellir (page 8) in 1798. Behind it is the stone **Dómkirkjan**, built by Christian VII when he replaced the Catholic church with a Lutheran one in 1796.

The old town expanded from Austurvöllur as far as Lækjargata and Fríkirkjuvegur to the east, and stretched from Hringbraut in the south to **Hafnarstræti** in the north. Hafnarstræti (Harbour Street) marked the watery edge of the city until the First World War, when gravel and sand were used to extend the waterfront.

The harbour area is full of touristy shops, and at the weekend the **Kolaportið** flea market teems with those in search of clothing bargains and Icelandic food specialities. Further along the shore to the east is Jón Gunnar Árnason's rather unlikely looking sculpture of a Viking ship.

A more prominent sculpture is that of the first settler Ingólfur, designed by Einar Jónsson. It crowns **Arnarhóll** (Eagle Hill) and overlooks the **Stjórnarráðið** (Government House), where the Prime Minister's office is found. Across the road is a cluster of mid-19th-century wooden buildings – the **Bernhöftstorfan** – where the **Tourist Information Centre** (page 61) can be found.

The main street of the old town is **Aðelstræti**. Its former workshops were developed in the 18th century by "the father of Reykjavík", Fógetinn (Sheriff) Skúli Magnússon, as a forward-thinking production initiative. His own weaving house was at no. 10.

To the south lies the **Tjörn**. At the corner, the **Ráðhús** (City Hall) squats solemnly like a watchman over skaters in the winter and people feeding the ducks in the summer. On the pond's eastern edge is the pretty

Stjórnarráðið

Lækjargata
⊕ Closed to the public.

Ráðhús

Corner of Tjarnagata and Vonarstræti
⊕ Closed to the public.

Listasafn Íslands

Frikirkjuvegur 7
☎ 562 1000
www.natgall.is
⊕ Tue-Sun: 11am-5pm.
Mon: closed.
Admission charge.
2 admissions for the price of 1 with voucher on page 63.

The Perlan

Fríkirkjan church.

The **Listasafn Íslands** (National Gallery), founded in 1884, is also here. The main building began life as an ice house storing ice cut from the Tjörn, which explains the thickness of the walls. It was later one of Reykjavík's most popular dance halls, but after a fire was turned into the gallery. It is chiefly concerned with frequently changing exhibitions of 19th- and 20th-century works, both Icelandic and foreign.

On the other side of the Tjörn, Suðurgata leads down past the **Þjóðminjasafn Íslands** (National Museum), which is closed for major renovations until June 2001.

The **Stofnun Árna Magnússonar** (Árni Magnússon Institute), also on Suðurgata, is a research institute named after a collector of medieval Icelandic manuscripts relating to the sagas and the Eddic poems. From June 2000 the special millennium exhibition of manuscripts – including *Eiríks saga rauða* (the saga of Eirik the Red) – will illuminate Iceland's conversion to Christianity one thousand years ago and the voyages of the Vikings to North America. *(Árnagarður, Suðurgata, ☎ 525 4010. ⏲ Tue-Sun: 9am-5pm. Mon: closed. Admission charge. 2 admissions for the price of 1 with voucher on page 63.)*

The nearby **Norræna Húsið** (Nordic House) was founded in 1968 to encourage Icelandic interest in other Nordic countries through its library of 30,000 Nordic books and its basement exhibition of arts and crafts. The building itself was designed by Finnish architect Alvar Aalto.

From here the futuristic splendour of the **Perlan** (The Pearl) is clearly visible. This revolving restaurant straddles the 24-million litre reservoirs on **Öskjuhlíð** (Ash Tree Hill), which cater for almost half the city's consumption of hot water straight

Norræna Húsið

4 · **A**

Sæmundargata
☎ 551 7030
⏲ Tue-Sun: 12noon-5pm.
Mon: closed.
Admission charge.
2 admissions for the price of 1 with voucher on page 63.

Kjarvalsstaðir

3 · **C**

Flókagötu
☎ 552 6131
www.reykjavik.is/listasafn
⏲ Mon-Sun: 10am-6pm.
Admission charge.
2 admissions for the price of 1 with voucher on page 63.

om the centre of the earth. An artificial
yser shoots water every five minutes for
e benefit of the diners.

orth of here is the **Kjarvalsstaðir**
Reykjavík Art Museum), whose exhibition
ace is dominated by the works of
hannes Kjarval (1885-1972). The
uilding also houses national and
ternational exhibitions of a wide variety
art, but the Erró paintings will be
oved to a new location near the harbour
om the spring of 2000. Allow time for a
ke in the café, with its spectacular view
Miklatún (Miklatún Park).

from most points of Reykjavík, the
allgrímskirkja is visible from here – in
ct, since its completion in 1974 it has
ted as a landmark for a 20km (12.5-
le) area. Even if you are not enamoured
the dramatic basalt structure, it is well
rth ascending the tower for an overview
the city. *(Skólavörðuholti, ☎ 510 1000.*
wer: May-Sep: Mon-Sun: 9am-6pm. Oct-Apr:
n-Sun: 9am-5pm. Admission charge. 2
missions for the price of 1 with voucher on
ge 63. Telephone for concert details.)

pposite the church is the **Safn Einars**
nssonar (Einar Jónsson Museum). It
ened in 1923 when the artist (1874-
54) also lived and worked here. He
ose the site and designed the building
mself, but his choice
s derided at the time by
ose in the old town who
clared that noone would
it a museum so far out
town. Iceland's first
ulptor produced a
olific amount of
intings and sculptures
his 60 years of work, all
which he donated to
e nation. On the top
or you can see the
eserved apartments he
ared with his wife.

ound the corner is the
tasafn ASÍ (Labour
ions Art Gallery),
ther museum located
a sculptor's former
ne, that of Ásmundur

Eiríksgata
☎ 551 3797
www.skulptur.is
🕐 Sep 15-Jun 1: Sat-Sun:
1.30pm-4pm. Mon-Fri:
closed. Jun 1-15 Sep:
Tue-Sun: 1.30pm-4pm.
Mon: closed.
Dec-Jan: closed.
Admission charge.
**2 admissions for the
price of 1 with voucher
on page 63.**

The view from the Hallgrímskirkja

Safn Ásgríms Jónssonar

Bergstaðastræti 74
☎ 562 1000, 551 3644
🕐 Jun-Aug: Tue-Sun:
1.30pm-4pm. Mon:
closed. Sep-May: open by
arrangement.
Admission charge.
2 admissions for the
price of 1 with voucher
on page 65.

Náttúrufræðistofnun Íslands

Hlemmur 3
☎ 562 9822
🕐 Jun-Aug: Sun, Tue, Thu,
Sat: 1pm-5pm. Sep-May:
Sun, Tue, Thu, Sat:
1.30pm-4pm. Mon, Wed,
Fri: closed.
Admission charge.
2 admissions for the
price of 1 with voucher
on page 65.

Ásmundarsafn

Sigtúni
☎ 553 2155
🕐 May-Sep: Mon-Sun:
10am-4pm. Oct-Apr:
Mon-Sun: 1pm-4pm.
Admission charge.
2 admissions for the
price of 1 with voucher
on page 65.

Sveinsson. The museum exhibits 20th-century paintings, sculptures and photographs from Iceland's most innovative contemporary artists. *(Freyjuga 41, ☎ 511 5353. 🕐 Tue-Sun: 2pm-6pm. Mon: closed. Admission charge. 2 admissions for th price of 1 with voucher on page 63.)*

Nearby is the **Safn Ásgríms Jónssonar** (Ásgrímur Jónsson Collection), found in the former studio home of this prolific landscape painter. This collection of oils, watercolours and drawings was bequeathed to the state upon his death.

On the waterside of the Hallgrímskirkja is the **Hið Íslenzka Reðasafn** (Icelandic Phallological Museum), which holds almost 100 penises and penile parts from Icelandic mammals, with the promise of human specimen from an immodest fan. Carvings of "penis" salt and pepper pots, napkin rings and toothpick holders are on sale. *(Laugavegur 24, ☎ 566 8668. 🕐 May-Aug: Tue-Sat: 2pm-5pm. Sun-Mon: closed. Sep-Apr: Tue, Sat: 2pm-5pm. Sun-Mon, Wed-Fri: closed. Admission charge. 2 admissions . the price of 1 with voucher on page 65.)*

Further along the road out of town is the **Náttúrufræðistofnun Íslands** (Icelandic Natural History Museum). This small but well-presented museum charts Icelandic geology, flora and fauna. There is also a mounted specimen of the Great Auk, a large non-flying bird that became extinct in 1844 as a result of over-hunting.

On the shoreline is **Höfði** (Höfði House), the municipal reception hall and site of the 1986 Reagan-Gorbachev summit. Th *Throne Pillars* sculpture outside is the work of Sigurjón Ólafsson.

Further along the windswept Laugarnes peninsula is the former studio of this outstanding, modernistic sculptor. After his death in 1982, the studio became th **Listasafn Sigurjóns Ólafssonar** (Sigurjón Ólafsson Museum), displaying his sculptures made from stone and concret bronze and wood. *(Laugarnesvegur 70, ☎ 553 2906. 🕐 Tue-Sun: 2pm-5pm. Mon: closed Admission charge. 2 admissions for the price 1 with voucher on page 65.)*

Turning inland brings you to an igloo-

Árbaer beneath the snow

...aped building that houses another
...culpture gallery, the **Ásmundarsafn**
...smundur Sveinsson Sculpture Museum).
...smundur Sveinsson's sculptures take their
...nspiration from the people, nature and
...agas of Iceland. Surrounding the building
...one of the artist's creations – is a garden
... his works cast in bronze and concrete.

...lso here in the Laugardalur valley is
...augardalslaug, the largest of the city's
...wimming baths. Here, visitors wallow in
...eland's allegedly healing geothermal
...ater – a delicious 29°C all year round.

...e **Fjölskyldu- og Húsdýragarðurinn**
...amily Park and Farm Animal Zoo) offers
...ble rides across a lake, a massive
...ndpit with rough-terrain vehicles, cycling
...d driving courses, remote-controlled
...ats and tests of strength. Among the
...imals found here are Icelandic horses
...d sheep, as well as cows, goats, mink,
...indeer, seals and salmon.

...ut of the city is the **Árbærsafn** (Árbær
...en-Air Museum), a cultural and
...chitectural recreation of Iceland's past.
...e historical houses and turf church
...ere relocated here from Reykjavík old
...wn and further afield, but the farm
...ildings stand on their original site. The
..."illage" is populated by costumed guides,
...ho run activities such as Haymaking Days.
...10 Reykjavík, ☎ 577 1111. ⏲ Jun-Aug: Mon:
...am-4pm. Tue-Fri: 9am-5pm. Sat-Sun: 10am-
...m. Aug-May: closed. Admission charge. *2 for
...e price of 1 with voucher on page 67.)*

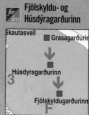

Fjölskyldu- og
Húsdýragarðurinn

Laugardalur
☎ 575 7800
⏲ Apr-Sep: Mon-Fri:
10am-6pm. Sat-Sun:
10am-5pm. Oct-Mar:
Wed: closed. Fjölskyldu
closed in winter.
Admission charge.
**2 admissions for the
price of 1 with voucher
on page 65.**

Laugardalslaug

Laugardalslaug
☎ 553 4039
⏲ Mon-Sun: 6.50am-
10.30pm.
Admission charge.
**2 admissions for the
price of 1 to any of the
seven swimming baths
listed on page 57 with
voucher on page 65.**

Reykjanes Peninsula

For most visitors the first glimpse of Iceland is the Reykjanes Peninsula, as **Keflavík** airport is situated right at its centre. In the dusk of a clear winter's day the view from the aircraft is breathtaking, and nicely in keeping with the widespread preconceptions about this sparsely populated country with its harsh climate.

The white expanse of the peninsula, dotted with the infrequent lights of small fishing communities, extends as far as the cliffs along its coast, where tentacles of ice stretch into the North Atlantic Ocean. In the steel-grey water itself, fishing vessels rise and fall, fragile and lonely.

In the summer the thick snow is replaced by a carpet of mosses, grasses and flowering plants. The 130km (80-mile) **Reykjavegur trail** from the Reykjanes lighthouse at the southeastern tip to the Nesjavellir power plant east of Reykjavík is one of the best walks in the country.

The promontory west of Keflavík is known as **Miðnes**. One of its tiny fishing communities is **Sandgerði**, where animal specimens, rocks and minerals are on view at the **Fræðasetrið í Sandgerði** (Nature Centre). The centre also offers guided tours around the nearby freshwater pond and along Sandgerði's 18km (11-mile) beach, and dolphin- and whale-watching trips with local fishermen.

Just off Route 41 lies **Grindavík** and the steaming cauldron of geothermal seawater in the middle of a lava field known as the

 Fræðasetrið í Sandgerði

Garðvegi 1, Sandgerði
☎ 423 7551
🕐 Jun–Aug: Mon–Fri: 9am–5pm. Sat–Sun: 1pm–5pm. Sep–May: Mon–Sun: 1pm–5pm.
Admission charge.
2 admissions for the price of 1 with voucher on page 67.

A bather relaxing in the warmth of the Blue Lagoon

Bláa Lonið (Blue Lagoon). The geothermal seawater is rich in a unique natural combination of minerals. The 40°C (104°F) temperature makes it popular for a refreshing soak with both Icelanders and tourists. Blue-green algae and white silica mud form a light natural sediment on the bottom of the lagoon, giving the water its soft, milky aquamarine appearance.

To the east is **Krísuvíkurbjarg**, Iceland's foremost cliffs for kittiwakes, and where fulmars, puffins and seals are also frequent visitors. The island of **Eldey** is an off-limits nature reserve and gannet colony attracting around 70,000 nesting birds each year.

Continuing east leads to **Strandarkirkja**. Legend decrees that this church was built by frightened sailors thankful to be delivered safely to shore. To the north are the bubbling mud pools of **Krísuvík** and the **Reykjanesfólkvangur** nature reserve. This vast 300sq-km (115sq-mile) expanse is dissected by a mesh of footpaths and pony trails. At its centre is **Kleifarvatn** lake, said to be home to a fearsome aquatic monster and quantities of trout.

The peninsula's most important settlement is **Hafnarfjörður**. Lying within the shadow of the capital, it nonetheless outshines Reykjavík in at least two respects. This town of 18,000 is actually the country's Viking centre, host to the international Viking Festival and site of Iceland's only Viking restaurant (page 49).

In addition, as a result of its location at the central point of several key natural energy lines, it is inhabited by many *Huldufólk* (hidden people). The *Huldufólk* are Adam and Eve's "hidden" children. God made them invisible when Eve denied their existence because she was ashamed that they were not clean. The construction of "human" roads and buildings is therefore restricted to areas known to be "unpopulated" by dwarves, gnomes, fairies and elves.

Along the picturesque waterfront is a warehouse housing the **Sjóminjasafn Íslands** (Maritime Museum), whose rowing boats, fishing tackle and ship miniatures chart the country's fishing history.

Bláa Lonið

Svartsengi, 240 Grindavik
☎ 4208800
www.bluelagoon.is
🕒 Open all year. Contact for seasonal opening hours.
Admission charge.
2 admissions for the price of 1 with voucher on page 67.

Sjóminjasafn Íslands

Vesturgata 8, 220 Hafnarfjörður
☎ 565 4242
🕒 Jun-Sep: Mon-Sun: 1pm-5pm. Oct-May: Sat-Sun: 1pm-5pm. Mon-Fri: closed.
Admission charge.
2 admissions for the price of 1 with voucher on page 67.

The snow-clad outskirts of Hafnarfjörður

Byggðasafn Hafnarfjarðar

☎ 565 5420
Sívertsens-húsið,
Vesturgata 6
🕐 Jun-Aug: Mon-Sun:
1pm-5pm. Sep-May:
Sat-Sun 1pm-5pm.
Siggubær, Kirkjuvegur 10
🕐 Jun-Aug: Sat-Sun:
1pm-5pm.
Smiðjan, Strandgata 50
🕐 May-Sep: Mon-Sun:
1pm-5pm.
Admission charge.
2 admissions for the
price of 1 with voucher
on page 67.

Hafnarborg

Strandgata 34
☎ 555 0080
🕐 Wed-Mon: 12noon-
6pm. Tue: closed.
Admission charge.
2 admissions for the price
of 1 with voucher on page 67.

Next door is one of three buildings belonging to the **Byggðasafn Hafnarfjarðar** (Hafnarfjörður Museum). The Sívertsens-húsið is the town's oldest building, built between 1803 and 1805, and has been sensitively renovated to show how an upper-class family would have lived. Siggubær (Sigga's House) is a complementary look at a working-class home. The Smiðjan (Smithy) is an annotated display of historical artefacts, from toys and tools to boats and barrels.

Since 1988 the **Hafnarborg** (Institute of Culture and Fine Art) has been the town's principal exhibition space, displaying works on different themes by national and foreign artists. The original building was donated to the town by the town chemist Sverrir Magnússon and his wife, both art enthusiasts, in 1983.

Bessastaðir was first recorded in the *Íslendiga Saga* (Saga of the Icelanders) by Sturla Þórðarson as home to Snorri Sturluson (page 9). It is now the presidential residence.

The inhabitants of **Kópavogur** swore allegiance to the Danish king in 1662 on pain of death, an event commemorated by the monument erected in 1962. Nearby are the lava formations of **Garðabær**.

West of Reykjavík is **Seltjarnarnes**, where stone house built in 1763 now houses the 9,000 artefacts of the **Nesstofusafn** (National Medical Museum). *(172 Seltjarnanes, ☎ 561 1016. 🕐 May-Sep: Tue, Thu, Sat-Sun: 1pm-5pm. Oct-Apr: closed. Admission charge.)*

South Central Iceland

Within easy reach of Reykjavík and Route 1 (the coastal Ring Road), and boasting some of the country's most publicized natural wonders, South Central Iceland is the country's most populated area. However, for many tourists the only glimpse of its attractions is on a whirlwind **Golden Circle** coach tour to Gulfoss and Geysir (page 56).

Equally accessible from the capital is the National Park of **Þingvellir**. This is the only place in Iceland to have been decreed a sacred place in law, on the grounds of its natural beauty, geological importance and historical relevance. The early settlers chose the site for their first national assembly in AD 930 and for the next three centuries – almost without interruption – the *Alþing* (Parliament) was to meet at the very point where the European and American tectonic plates pull apart.

Þingvellir

The great **Almannagjá** fissure – home to Þingvellir's protective spirit, Ármann – runs beneath the lava plain along the northern shore of the lake of Þingvallavatn. The vikings diverted the Öxará river to flow through the fissure to make a more dramatic backdrop to the *Alþing*.

An Icelandic flag indicates the site of the **Lögberg** (Law Rock), below, where the lögrétta (legislature) of *goðar*, or chieftains, convened to formulate new laws. The spot was no doubt chosen for the quality of its acoustics, for it was here that the lögsögumaður (lawspeaker) declared the country's rules out loud. The stones that surround the Lögberg are the remains of búðir, or booths, erected by the participating goðar each year as temporary shelters for the two-week duration of the *Alþing*.

Þingvallakirkja

Covering 84sq km (30sq miles), **Þingvallavatn** is one of the country's largest lakes. On its eastern shore is the church of **Þingvallakirkja**. The current church dates from the 19th century, although this was also the site for the first church to be consecrated in Iceland.

Continuing east past **Laugarvatn** – a warm lake popular with windsurfers – brings visitors to the site of the celebrated **Geysir** that first exploded in 1294. The name-

Geysir

Gulfoss

Gulfoss

Kjölur

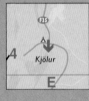

Langjökull

giving geyser sadly no longer erupts, but its neighbour **Strokkur** can be relied upon to spout to a height of about 20m (66ft) every few minutes. Until it was recently prohibited, Geysir was made to erupt each year on Independence Day by force-feeding it soap powder to lower the temperature of the surface water. Natural eruptions occur when boiling water deep below the surface explodes through the cooler water above. Injuries sustained by tourists curious to test the temperature of the bubbling mud pools are surprisingly common.

Just a few minutes drive away is Iceland's other major tourist attraction, **Gulfoss**. Here the Hvitá river plunges 32m (105ft) into a massive canyon 2.5km (1.5 miles) long. In the summer there is likely to be a rainbow; in the winter when the falls are frozen, the effect is equally impressive.

Since 1975 this natural wonder has been a government nature reserve, but its future was not always secure. At the beginning of the century there were plans by foreign investors to use the falls for a massive hydroelectric development. That these plans were not implemented is largely due to the canvassing of a local farmer's daughter, Sigríður Tómasdóttir, whose achievement is commemorated in the small museum above the falls.

Those with their own four-wheel-drive vehicles may choose to investigate the black and barren plains of the uninhabited interior by the **Kjölur** route, one of the oldest and most crowded (in relative terms of course) tracks across the interior. The stone and gravel track to the glacial lake of **Hagavatn** and the **Langjökull** ice cap is torturously uneven. The section nearest the ice cap is accessible only by foot but the fantastic view of the lake below is worth the wind's buffeting. More spectacular still s the view of the larger glacial lake **Hvitárvatn**, to the east.

Hvitárvatn

From here, continue to the hot springs and bubbling mud pools of **Hveravellir**, where the interior's only permanent residents man the meteorological station. Alternatively, if the rains have been heavy – which can make the river impassable – take a detour to **Kerlingarfjöll**, where lush hills and rhyolite slopes make a welcome contrast to the flat and dour monotony of Kjölur.

Kerlingarfjöll

Many of the Golden Circle tours progress from Gulfoss to **Skálholt**, Iceland's first Christian bishopric and a site of great historical and religious importance. The first church was built here by the holy man Gissur the White, whose son Ísleifur became Iceland's first bishop in 1053. Ísleifur's son continued where his father left off, introducing the tithe to help finance the church, the poor, and the schools that established Skálholt as Iceland's foremost educational centre.

A monument near the present church was erected in memory of the Catholic bishop Jón Arason and his two sons, who were beheaded here for opposing the Reformation in the 16th century. Skálholt's decline into near obscurity came when the centre of the Icelandic church moved to Reykjavík in 1797. The present church was begun in 1954.

Skálholt

To the east lies **Þjórsárdalur**, squarely within the shadow of fearsome **Hekla**, a mountain once widely thought to be the mouth of Hell. In 1104 this fearsome volcano erupted, burying the valley and its scattered farmsteads beneath a torrent of ash. Excavations in 1939 uncovered the remains of the Viking longhouse at **Stöng**, which was used as the inspiration for the

Hveravellir

Fjallabak

reconstruction built at nearby **Þjóðveldisbær** in 1974.

Another volcanically active area, though not as recently active as Mount Hekla (which last erupted in February 2000), lies to the southeast in the **Fjallabak** nature reserve. **Landmannalaugar** is difficult to miss, not least because of the steam swirling up from its hot pools. They are justifiably popular with bathers, because the combination of geothermal water and cool spring water makes the temperature perfect.

Eldgjá

The choice of hikes is endless, and weird and wonderful lava flows, softly undulating mountains of rhyolite rock and breathtaking views abound. As rhyolite erodes, it takes on a whole palette of colours, so the hills alternate in an aesthetic display from oranges and reds to greens and creams.

The Kerið crater at sunset

From here it is an easy and rewarding trip to **Eldgjá** (Fire Gorge), the world's largest fissure at 18km (11 miles) long, 500m (1,640ft) wide and 150m (500ft) deep. Plunging into the fissure is the **Ófærufoss** waterfall.

Þórisvatn

The track north of Landmannalaugar passes the nation's second largest lake, **Þórisvatn**. The black gravel plains continue uninterrupted as far as **Nýidalur**, where there is a scattering of warm and cosy huts for the hardy walkers who come here. Still further, beyond the ice cap **Tungnafellsjökull** are the warm springs of

Laugafell, which mark the start of the gravel plains of **Sprengisandur**.

If your interest leans more towards the coast than the interior, leave Reykjavík by Route 1, also known as the Ring Road. The first point of interest is then **Hveragerði**, nicknamed Iceland's "greenhouse village". This area offers wonderful hiking opportunities. One of its appeals is that the earth literally breathes with bubbling hot springs. This heat has been harnessed in a massive geothermal horticultural project, enabling coffee, bananas, asparagus and mandarins to be grown. **Eden** is one of the greenhouse marvels that is open to the public.

Just to the north of the town in the **Gufudalur** steam valley are the hot springs of **Gryla**, named after the malcontent mother of the 13 *jólasveinarn*, or Christmas lads. According to pagan tradition, the boys take it in turns to leave a gift in each child's shoe left on the windowsill on the 13 nights before Christmas. If children have been naughty, they are left a potato. Really bad children are told to expect a visit from Gryla herself, who with her three eyes and terrible warts thought nothing of snacking on naughty children.

On the coast is **Þorlákshöfn** harbour, departure point for the **Vestmannaeyjar** (Westmann Islands) ferry. If the *Landnámabók* (Book of Settlements) is to be believed the early history of this small group of islands is a rather inauspicious one. Evidently, they were first unsuccessfully occupied by a group of Irish slaves who fled here after murdering their master, Hjörleifur, the brother of Ingólfur Arnarson at Hjörleifshöfði (page 27). Their hiding place was discovered, however, and they in turn were brutally murdered for their sins.

The islands are still visited today by those wishing to get away from it all. Only the largest island, **Heimaey**, has a permanent population – permanent as long as the land allows, that is. In 1973, the eastern side of the island was suddenly engulfed in lava from a subglacial volcano. Not a single life was lost, but it took six months

Tungnafellsjökull

Hveragerði

Þorlákshöfn

Vestmannaeyjar

**Fiska- og
Náttúrugripasafn
Vestmannæyja**

Heiðarveg 12, Heimaey
☎ 481 1997
www.vestmannaeyjar.is/
safnahus/natturu.htm
🕓 May-Sep: Mon-Sun:
11am-5pm. Oct-Apr:
Sat-Sun: 3pm-5pm.
Mon-Fri: closed.
Admission charge.

Ingólfsfjall

Á Njáluslóð

Hvolsvöllur
☎ 487 8781
njala@islandia.is
🕓 Open by arrangement.

of pumping water over the 5 million sq m of lava before the eruption was declared over and residents could return home.

The **Fiska- og Náttúrugripasafn Vestmannæyja** (Aquarium and Natural History Museum) in Heimaey town is worth a look for its mounted nesting birds, its rock and minerals and its tanks of fish.

Most of the Vestmannaeyjar were created a mere 5,000 years ago, and **Surtsey**, the sixteenth addition to this motley island family was born as late as 1963. It was named after the tempestuous Norse giant Surtur. The island is closed to the public as scientists excitedly chart all its geological formations.

Continuing along the Ring Road from Hveragerði brings you into the heart of Iceland's richest farming area. The main town here is **Selfoss**. Just before the town is the mountain of **Ingólfsfjall**, according to legend the last resting-place of Ingólfur Arnarson (page 8). The area is pock-marked by craters. The most impressive is **Kerið**, a 55m (180-ft) basin formed by a blast 3,000 years ago.

Further east towards Oddi lies an area of great importance for the sagas. This is where that important 13th-century work, the *Njáls Saga*, is believed to have been set. The farmhouse of the principal character, Njáll, is **Bergþórshvoll**, to the south of the Ring Road.

Archaeological finds uncovered in the 1920s and 1950s lend credence to the burning of Njáll's farm and family described in the saga. This thrilling and complex tale, covering 50 years of bloodshed and feuding, loyalty and honour, is looked at in some detail at the **Á Njáluslóð** (Saga Centre).

The town of **Oddi** itself is revered as the sometime home of a number of those responsible for recording the sagas. East of the main road is the popular wooded glacial valley of **Þórsmörk** (Thor's Forest). This seemingly impenetrable pocket of birch, willow and wild flowers is penned in by clear rivers, snowy mountains and impressive glaciers, and can be reached only by a precarious dirt track.

Despite this inaccessibility – or perhaps because of it – on fine weekends there are plenty of groups treading the path to viewpoints over the glaciers and ice caps, including **Eyjafjallajökull**, which borders Þórsmörk to the south. Throughout the summer, the huts and campsites are full and the biggest of the track's numerous river crossings are congested with tour buses and four-wheel-drive land cruisers.

The Ring Road leads on to **Skógar** and the **Skógafoss** waterfall. Tradition states that the settler Þrasi hid a chest of gold under the 60m (195ft) waterfall. Between mid-July and early September hikers tread a path from Skógar to Þórsmörk through the **Fimmvörðuháls** pass, which threads between the ice caps of Eyjafjallajökull and **Mýrdalsjökull**.

Skógar

Mýrdalsjökull is the icy home of the **Katla** sub-glacial volcano, whose next eruption is considered long overdue. In winter, skiers rather than walkers populate the area. At **Dyrhólaey** a photogenic arch of rock juts out of the sea, and puffin and arctic terns crowd the sheer cliffs.

Kötlutangi

Despite its claim to be Iceland's wettest spot, **Vík** is widely considered one of the world's best beaches. Rugged cliffs populated by nesting seabirds overlook the wide black sand beaches attacked by the raging surf of the North Atlantic. Look seawards and poking out of the sea are the **Reynisdrangur**, gnarled black pillars of rock where arctic terns nest. Turn landwards and the bleak cliffs are enveloped by a cloak of green hills, topped by the Mýrdalsjökull ice cap.

The rocky fingers of Reynisdrangur

To the east is **Kötlutangi**, Iceland's southernmost point, and to the north is **Hjörleifshöfði**, where Ingólfur Arnarson's brother Hjörleifur was murdered.

Southeast Iceland

A small lake at the snout of one of the Vatnajökull glaciers

Vatnajökull

Laki

Kirkjubæjarklaustur

The southeast of Iceland hides some of the country's most hauntingly remote and wildly inaccessible parts. Before the Ring Road was extended in 1974, areas of the coast, such as the town of Höfn (page 30), could only be reached by driving down from the north, which meant that a drive to Reykjavík had to go via the north coast.

The reason for this impenetrability is simple – ice. The largest ice cap in Europe, **Vatnajökull**, is located here. Vatnajökull's glaciers wriggle like icy blue fingers between craggy mountain ribs, and the seething volcanoes beneath vomit up bilious torrent of undigested debris and melted ice with alarming regularity.

One of the most talked-about eruptions in the area was born from the now extinct **Laki** craters in 1783. The ten-month eruption produced a mammoth 30 billion tonnes of rocky lava and a gas so noxious that a fifth of the human population and half of the animal population died. The effect was devastating and long lasting, and ruined and deserted farms can still be seen in the area.

The town of **Kirkjubæjarklaustur**, meaning "the church farm convent", was miraculously spared. Apparently the tireless flow of lava was brought to a dramatic standstill at **Eldmessutangi** (Fire Sermon Point) where pastor Jón Steingrímsson preached his *eldmessa* (fire sermon) before a transfixed congregation.

The religious significance of this town

predates this fortuitous event, however. The first Norse settler was a Christian, Ketill the Foolish. He prophesied that pagans would meet disaster here, which certainly proved true for the unfortunate Hildur Eysteinsson, who dropped down dead at a point now marked by the **Hildishaugar** rock to the east of town. In the 12th century a Benedictine nunnery was founded here, although it was disbanded during the 16th-century Reformation.

Crossing the interminable *sandur*, or sand desert, of **Skeiðarásandur** requires great care. The damage to the bridges and Ring Road caused by the floods in the wake of the 1996 eruption of Vatnajökull's **Grímsvötn** volcanic crater has now been repaired, but debilitating sandstorms are an ever-present concern.

Skeiðarásandur

The main pull for visitors to southeast Iceland is the **Skaftafell** National Park, first established in 1967 and later extended in 1984 to include about 20% of Vatnajökull itself. Ask at the tourist centre at the base of the slope for details of the numerous walks that can be made to its various gullies and glaciers, crevices and canyons, waterfalls and valleys. The trails all leave from the car park, and invariably take in at least part of the rich plant and bird life to be found here, from wild angelica and wood sorrel to skuas, wrens and redwings.

Skaftafellsjökull

Svartifoss

One of the most popular trails, along which you can reasonably expect to make friends with the streams of fellow walkers, is the two-hour return trail to the treacherously slippery glacier **Skaftafellsjökull**. A walk of similar duration to the west of the camping area leads to the **Svartifoss** waterfall, with the option to continue to the Sjónarsker peak, or still further to a viewpoint overlooking the twin glaciers of Morsárjökull and Skaftafellsjökull.

The promontory **Ingólfshöfði**,

Svartifoss in Skaftafell National Park

Höfn Glacier Tours

☎ 478 1000

across the shallow water from the mainland, was a temporary home to the settler Ingólfur Arnarson while he waited for the pillars of his high seat to ordain the location of the first settlement (page 12).

Continuing along the Ring Road brings you to the stunning deep glacial lake of **Jökulsárlón**, location for the opening scenes of the James Bond film *A View to a Kill*. The lake is fed from the **Breiðamerkurjökull** glacier, which is currently unable to drain into the sea as a result of shifts in the surrounding land.

The port of Seyðisfjörður

For a closer look at the beautifully sculpted icebergs calved from the glacier take a boat cruise on the lake.

Beyond the wetlands teeming with water birds lies **Höfn**. This unexceptional fishing and fish-processing town is found in an exceptional setting crowning the Hornafjörður fjord. Its concrete buildings aside, it is of interest to tourists primarily as the starting point for the popular summer Glacier Tours, which include boat excursions on Jökulsárlón and snowmobile runs across Kverkfjöll (page 32).

Lónsöræfi

For those in search of yet more hiking opportunities, the nature reserve of **Lónsöræfi** surrounding Höfn offers a plethora of valleys and gorges gouged from the mountains by the Jökulsá river. Overnight stays are possible at the Stafafell farm. It is worth sticking around to explore the Lón lagoon, particularly for the nesting swans at its eastern end.

The island across from the small village of Djúpivogur is called **Papey**, after the Irish monks who are said to have first lived there. Its tiny, wooden church – built at the beginning of the 19th century – is said to be the oldest in the country.

The scenic coastal road, separating the chaos of the North Atlantic from the regal mountains behind, twists between the little-visited villages of the East Fjords. **Reyðarfjörður**, **Eskifjörður** and **Neskaupstaður** are the most remarkable for their (marginally) more prosperous harbours.

Easily the largest and wealthiest settlement to grace this wild stretch of coast is **Seyðisfjörður**, the entry port for ferries from Europe. Perhaps not surprisingly, many of the buildings exhibit a Norwegian influence.

A short drive inland brings the ferry's new arrivals beyond the charm contained within the green slopes that encircle Seyðisfjörður to the bland modernity of **Egilsstaðir**, built in the middle of the 20th century as the hub of all the main roads in the east.

The **Minjasafn Austurlands** (East Iceland Heritage Museum) portrays the life, culture and work of the region from settlement in the early Middle Ages to the present day. The artefacts include items from a pagan grave and the restored living quarters of an old Icelandic farm.

Immediately to the south of the town lies the **Lögurinn** lake. Tales of the fearsome serpent lurking beneath its glassy green surface and the attractive dense wood of dwarf birch and mountain ash on its eastern shore combine to attract large numbers of campers each year. The trees were planted by the forestry commission as part of much-needed reforestation.

Near the southern end of the lake is a short but challenging trail to the thundering "hanging falls" of **Hengifoss**, which plunge 118m (390ft) down a brown- and pink-striped gorge. At the southernmost tip of Lögurinn is the church of **Valþjófsstaður**, whose door was carved with a battle scene around 1200.

Minjasafn Austurlands

Laufskógar 1,
700 Egilsstaðir
☎ 471 1412
🕘 Jun-Aug: Tue-Sun:
11am-5pm. Mon: closed.
Sep-May: Fri: 1pm-5pm
and other times by
arrangement.
Admission charge.
**2 admissions for the
price of 1 with voucher
on page 67.**

Lögurinn

Hengifoss

Herðubreið

Reached only by several jolting hours over the rugged terrain of **Fljótsdalsheiði** (River Valley Moors) in a four-wheel-drive vehicle is the extinct volcano **Snæfell** (Snow Mountain). Aside from the occasional lake, the route's only distraction is the possibility of seeing herds of wild reindeer. There is a hut at the base of the peak, from where it is a hard six-hour slog to the summit 1,000m (3,280ft) further up.

West of Snæfell and north of Vatnajökull are the geothermal Kverkfjöll (Nook Mountains, below), which are best reached by returning to Egilsstaðir and taking first the Ring Road and then the southbound track just beyond Grímsstaðir.

The route undulates through harsh black hills almost as far as the symmetrical mountain of **Herðubreið**, which rises imposingly to a height of 1,060m (3,500ft) from a flat plain. The first climb to the summit was made in 1908, and today determined climbers with proper equipment can leave the warden's hut in Herðubreiðarlindir and reach the summit along the western slope in a single long summer's day.

Vikursandur

Between Herðubreið and Askja the sandy coloured pumice dunes of **Vikursandur** dominate the landscape. This breathtaking 50sq km (19sq mile) caldera was created by an eruption in 1875, as was the hot Vit lake at its northeastern edge. Movement did not finally finish until some thirty years later, however, when a further collapse of material resulted in the formation of the brilliant blue **Öskjuvatn** lake, which at 217m (715ft) is the nation's deepest lake.

Dyngjujökull

Gæsavatnaleið is the tricky route extending southwest of Askja as far as the **Dyngjujökull** glacier, which is black due to its shawl of black ash. The bumpy terrain is notorious for dangerous flooding and should only be attempted by experienced four-wheel drivers.

Kverkfjöll

The track between Herðubreiðarlindir and Askja leads to the **Kverkfjöll** mountains themselves. Dominating the mountain range is the Kverkfjöll volcano, the second-highest volcano in the country. In the same area are the smoking "hot

prings valley" of **Hveradalur**, and the
amed ice caves that dramatically steam
nd melt as a result of the boiling water of
he Jökulsá á Kverkfjöll river flowing
eneath them.

Heading north out of Egilsstaðir along
Route 94 eventually returns to the coast at
Borgarfjörður, also known as Bakkagerði.
This remote outpost is primarily
emembered as the birthplace of the artist
Jóhannes Kjarval (1885-1972), who
ainted the church's altarpiece.

Húsey

Norður Héra, Egilsstaðir
☎ 471 3010

Kverkfjöll

lternatively, Route 925 running north
om Egilsstaðir leads to an out-of-the-way
arm banked on the flatlands south of the
ökulsá á Dal river. The **Húsey** farm and
outh Hostel encapsulates the isolation
nd serenity of Iceland. It is a perfect
etreat for birdwatchers, horse riders and
hilosophers.

ollowing the Jökulsá á Dal and Route
23 southwards leads to the farm of
Aðalból, where Viking remains are thought
belong to the *Hrafnkels Saga*.
ccording to this typically complex tale the
entral character set in motion a spiral of
loodthirstiness and revenge when he
wore to Freyr, the Norse god of war, to
nd the life of anyone who rode his
avourite horse without permission. In
ontrast with modern notions of justice
nd morality, the thoroughly undeserving
nd vicious Hrafnkel ends his days
eacefully, enjoying health and wealth.

Aðalból

Aðalból 1
☎ 471 1071

Northeast Iceland

Minjasafnið Burstarfell

Vopnafjörður
☎ 473 1466
🕒 Jun-Sep: Mon-Sun:
10am-7pm. Oct-May:
closed.
Admission charge.

Vopnafjörður

Langanes

Few are prepared to battle with the poor transport links and mediocre tourist services in the remote northeast, despite the ample rewards. The tiny, untouched villages along its ragged coast embrace the visitor to the heart of an authentic fisherman's Iceland. The main reason for the isolation is that the Ring Road cuts straight from Egilsstaðir (page 31) to Mývatn (page 37), leaving the coast accessible only by the lesser Route 85.

Mývatn is one of the region's highlights, along with the equally unspoilt Jökulsárgljúfur National Park. Just below the Arctic Circle, this corner of the country is generally cooler and drier than the south.

Turning towards the coast from Egilsstaðir, the road passes two lakes – there is a fine viewing platform at the first, **Nýkurvatn** – before coming to **Burstarfell**. An 18th-century turf farmhouse now houses an informative folk museum, **Minjasafnið Burstarfell**.

Once at the coast, the first town is **Vopnafjörður**. This small town is pretty but unremarkable, except that is as the birthplace of a former Miss World. It is also supposedly the home town of Father Christmas, who is said to stay on **Smjörfjöll** (Butter Mountain) to the south when not making his seasonal deliveries.

To the north is the **Langanes** peninsula, a bleak and impenetrable tongue of land, fringed on all sides by high cliffs and fog. Many of its farms have been abandoned, but the peninsula is still inhabited by gannets. At the inland end of the peninsula is the sheltered harbour and trading centre of **Þórshöfn**. There is a cross at **Fontur** the tip of the peninsula, to

Burstarfell

ndicate where shipwrecked English sailors are said to have climbed up the sheer cliffs.

The northernmost village in Iceland is **Raufarhöfn**, where the sun doesn't set for a whole month in the summer. In the winter it is comparably bleak. Until the recent addition of an airport near the village, it was completely inaccessible except by sea during the long, dark winter months.

Raufarhöfn

n its heyday in the 1950s, Raufarhöfn was one of Iceland's major salting and processing centres for herring. Despite appearing to successfully make the move from herring to cod after the change in herring migration patterns, the village lost its former economic status.

Jökulsárgljúfur

Just above the village is the lighthouse of **Hraunhafnartangi**, the actual northernmost point of the mainland. On the other side of the flat and windswept peninsula of **Melrakkaslétta** the road takes in the tiny village of **Kópasker** (population a mere 160), before continuing to the turn-off to **Jökulsárgljúfur** National Park. The park borders the Jökulsá á Fjöllum river, whose source is the Kverkfjöll mountains (page 32).

Dettifoss

The park greets visitors with the impressive **Ásbyrgi** canyon. Findings by geologists indicate that the canyon is the result of a glacial flow set in motion by an eruption under the Vatnajökull ice cap, but the Viking explanation is more fun. They claimed that the canyon was the hoofprint of the god Odin's flying horse.

From the information office a path ascends the 60m (200ft) to the top of the canyon. From here you can continue to the bizarre basalt pinnacles of **Hljóðaklettar**, or Echoing Rocks, which have been sculpted naturally by the river. If you walk for a full two days you will come to the park's highlight, the deafening waterfall of **Dettifoss**. The falls are so massive – 500 cu m (17,655 cu ft) of water tumble over a depth of 44m (145ft) every second – that the resulting cloud of spray can be seen from several kilometres away.

Dettifoss

Returning to Route 85 and the mouth of

Stream flowing out of Mývatn

Tjörnes

Safnahúsið á Húsavík

Stóragarði 17,
640 Húsavík
☎ 464 1860
www.landvist.is/
safnahusid/
⏰ Jun-Aug: Mon-Sun:
10am-6pm. Sep-May:
Mon-Fri: 9am-12noon,
1pm-5pm. Sun: 4pm-6pm.
Sat: closed.
Admission charge.
2 admissions for the
price of 1 with voucher
on page 69.

the Öxarfjörður fjord, the road to the west
sweeps by Garður and the Víkingavatn lake
before flowing past the cliffs of the
Tjörnes peninsula. The Ytritunga fossil
beds here give important clues as to the
warmer climate Iceland enjoyed in a
previous age. The western edge of Tjörnes
offers good views of **Flatey** ("Flat Island")
and **Lundey** ("Puffin Island") in Skjálfandi
bay.

Húsavík was actually the first place in
Iceland to be permanently settled, but the
haphazard nature of this settlement has
denied it the prestige associated with the
claim. A Swedish Viking and his entourage
spent a winter here, but at their departure
in spring, a few tardy slaves were
mistakenly left behind.

The archives, photographs and paintings
at the **Safnahúsið á Húsavík** (Folk
Museum) build a picture of what life was
like here in times past. Amid the birds,
fish, seals, minerals and plants is one
exhibit that everyone wants to see – a
stuffed polar bear that was killed on the
island of Grímsey in 1969. In 2001 a new
building housing maritime exhibits will
open.

Húsavík's cross-shaped church with its
immense 26m (85ft) spire boasts an
altarpiece for which the local painter
Sveinn Þórarinsson used town residents as
models. The road south of the town is
lined with racks for drying fish, a clear

indication of the primary occupation of the northeast's most important town.

Grenjaðarstaður is a brief diversion on the way south to Mývatn. In the 19th century this manor farm (turf house) was the largest and best in the area, providing a home for some 30 people. Since 1958 the restored farm rooms – including the pantry, kitchen, bedrooms, storerooms and the local post office – have become the local **Byggðasafn** (Folk Museum).

If travellers to the northeast come to just one place it is invariably **Mývatn** (Midge Lake). The swarms of midges are insufficient deterrent to the hordes of walkers drawn to explore the volcanic and geothermal treasures in the Mývatn basin.

Straddling the Mid-Atlantic Ridge this broad and shallow lake has more than 50 islands and, at breeding times, is populated by tens of thousands of birds.

On the lake's northeastern shore is **Reykjahlíð**, a settlement sustained jointly by tourism, the Bjarnarflag diatomite plant and the Krafla geothermal power station.

The area around Mývatn is one of the most volcanically volatile on earth, and subterranean activity is frequently recorded. The most recent series of eruptions in 1981-84 is called the Kralfa Fires after its source, the nearby mountain **Krafla**. They were preceded by the Mývatn Fires in 1724-29, when the rivers of lava actually parted to spare the church which then stood in Reykjahlíð.

Possible day excursions from Reykjahlíð include hiking to the large crater of Hverfell and searching the unique craters of **Dimmuborgir** for its famous population of *Huldufólk* (page 19). There is also the active lava field of **Leirhnjúkur**, the crater lake of **Víti** (source of the Mývatn Fires), and Krafla.

Several tours take in the **Námaskarð** geothermal area, the spitting mudpools of Hverarond (watch out for your shoes!), and the diatomite plant and potato fields of Bjarnarflag, as well as Víti, Leirhnjúkur and Krafla. Birdwatchers should head to Laxá.

for less **Byggðasafn á Grenjaðarstaður**

Grenjaðarstaður
☎ 881 2435
🕐 Jun-Aug: Mon-Sun: 10am-6pm. Sep-May: closed.
Admission charge.
2 admissions for the price of 1 with voucher on page 69.

Mývatn

Reykjahlíð

Krafla

North Central Iceland

Laufás

Grýtubakkahreppi,
610 Grenivík
☎ 463 3106
🕒 Jun-15 Sep: Mon-Sun:
10am-6pm.
16 Sep-May: closed.
Admission charge.

Lystigarðurinn

Eyrarlandsholti 3, Akureyri
☎ 462 7487
🕒 Jun-Oct: Mon-Fri:
8am-10pm. Sat-Sun:
9am-10pm.
Nov-May: closed.
Admission free.

Sigurhæðir

Eyrarandsvegi 3, Akureyri
☎ 462 6648
🕒 15 Jun-Aug: Tue-Fri:
2pm-4pm. Sep-14 Jun:
open by arrangement.
Admission charge.

The Ring Road runs through central Iceland's pretty agricultural land to the north of the interior, so if you stick to it you join the majority of tourists who miss out on the stunning coastal scenery of the northern fjords. Although they may be wild and lacking in facilities, the dirt tracks along the coast offer a feast of birds and beaches.

While still on the Ring Road, the first stopping point when journeying from the east is **Goðafoss** (Falls of the Gods). According to the sagas this waterfall acquired its name when Þorgeir of Ljósavatn – *lögsögumaður* (lawspeaker) at the *Alþing* – hurled his statues of the gods into it when Iceland converted to Christianity in the year 1000.

At the coastal junction, the road banks north for the illuminating **Laufás** (Farm Museum) and the attractive fishing village of **Grenivík**, or continues south to **Akureyri**. With a growing population of 15,000, Akureyri has been a leading trading centre since its origins in the early 17th century, and its factories, breweries, shipyards and shops continue to thrive.

The climate is enviable – in the summer there is sun and in the winter there is snow. Almost all the indigenous Icelandic plants that can grow in the region's fertile soil are displayed at the **Lystigarðurinn** (Botanical Garden).

While much of the town is unbearably modern – not least the 1940's basalt church designed by the same architect as Reykjavík's Hallgrímskirkja (page 15), Gudjón Samúelsson – enough of the older houses have been preserved to retain an air of traditional charm. The oldest is **Laxdalshús**, built as a Danish trading house in 1795.

Old buildings open to the public as museums include **Sigurhæðir**, the home of the author of Iceland's national anthem, poet Matthías Jochumsson, and **Davíðshús**, the home of the writer Davíð Stefánsson. *(Bjarkarstíg 6, ☎ 962 1498.* 🕒 *Jun-Aug: Mon-Sun: 3pm-6pm. Sep-May: open by arrangement. Admission charge.)*

Nonnahús (Nonni's House) is the childhood home of Jón Sveinsson (1857-1944), the Jesuit priest and writer of children's books under the pseudonym Nonni. The museum contains his books in many languages, photos and documents.

On the same street is the **Minjasafnið á Akureyri** (Akureyri Museum), where objects and photos from times past to the present day are preserved. Display items include tools, typewriters and milk cartons.

Other attractions include the **Náttúrufræðustifnun** (Natural History Museum) and the **Listasafn Akureyrar** (Akureyri Art Museum).

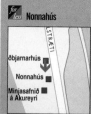

for less **Nonnahús**

Aðalstræti 54, Akureyri
☎ 462 3555
⏰ Jun-Aug: Mon-Sun:
10am-5pm. Sep-May:
open by arrangement.
Admission charge.
**2 admissions for the
price of 1 with voucher
on page 69.**

Akureyri

Reached by air or sea from Akureyri is the island of **Grímsey**, whose location on the Arctic Circle means extreme weather and a hardy population. The environment obviously suits the feathered community, however, as the island's 100 permanent residents are massively outnumbered by the 36 different species of bird that nest on Grímsey's northern and eastern shores.

If birds are not of interest, it is not hard to find a local willing to tell tales about the island's first settler, the Viking Grímur, or its more recent American benefactor, the chess champion Daniel Willard Fiske. Fiske donated firewood, books and chess sets to the island after hearing of its passion for chess.

To the northwest is the **Kolbeinsey** rock, the point from which Iceland measures

for less **Minjasafnið á
Akureyri**

Aðalstræti 58, Akureyri
☎ 462 4162
⏰ Jun-Sep: Mon-Sun:
11am-5pm. Oct-May:
Sun: 2pm-4pm.
Mon-Sat: closed.
Admission charge.
**2 admissions for the
price of 1 with voucher
on page 69.**

Grímsey from above

the boundaries of its waters.

Back on the mainland, there are several possible excursions from Akureyri. The mountain visible from the town is **Mount Súlur**, and its summit can be reached in several hours. During the ski season, crowds flock to nearby slopes at **Hlíðarfjall**. Route 821 south takes in a geriatric hospital at Kristnes which was the first large building to use geothermal heating, the protected church at Grund and the typical turf and stone church at nearby Saurbær.

Just over 10km (6 miles) north of Akureyri is the **Safnasafnið** (Folk Art Museum), a unique museum with old-fashioned gardens opened in 1998 in a former school overlooking Eyjafjörður. The paintings, sculptures, embroideries, models, drawings, toys and tools present an informative and clever look at modern art and the stimuli that lie behind it.

Route 82 runs through the fishing town of **Dalvík**. The town is visited less for its own sake and more as a base for walking or horse riding through the scenic snow fields of **Heljardalsheiði**, or to catch a ferry to the island of **Hrísey**. At 8km (5 miles) long and 2.5km (1.5 miles) wide, Hrísey is Iceland's second largest island.

On the headland of **Olafsfjarðarmúli** is the village of **Ólafsfjörður**, which is reached by a single lane 3.4km (2-mile) tunnel through the mountainside.

A rather circuitous road leads to another coastal community, **Siglufjörður**, a former

Náttúrufræðustífnun

Hafnarstræti 81, Akureyri
☎ 462 2983
⏰ Jun–Aug: Mon–Sun: 10am–5pm. Sep–May: open on request.
Admission charge.

Listasafn Akureyrar

Kaupvangsstræti 24, Akureyri
☎ 461 2610
⏰ Tue–Thu, Sun: 2pm–6pm. Fri–Sat: 2pm–10pm.
Mon: closed.
Admission charge.

centre of the herring industry until the fish disappeared from the area in 1970. Now it is a tourist town for skiers. It boasts a dramatic location within the arms of steep mountains overlooking a beautiful fjord.

The **Síldarminjasafnid** (Herring Era Museum) is found in the building where seasonal workers lived and worked during the herring boom. Through tools, artefacts and special summer shows, the museum recreates the era that was so instrumental in the development of modern Iceland.

At the fascinating **Vesturfarasetrið** (Icelandic Emigration Centre) in **Hofsós**, visitors can learn about the mass exodus of one-fifth of Iceland's population to the New World between 1870 and 1914.

Nestled within the sheer mountains inland is **Hólar**, a prosperous bishopric from 1106 and home to an Agricultural College since 1882. The impressive **Hólakrikja** (Cathedral) only dates from 1763, but inside are some wonderful pre-Reformation ecclesiastical treasures. It is particularly proud to have in its possession the first-ever Icelandic translation of the Bible, printed in 1584.

Beneath the Skagafjörður fjord, in the heart of this region's rich farmland, is the **Byggðasafn Skagfirðinga** (Glaumbær Museum). The museum recreates rural Iceland in centuries past with its traditional turf and timber buildings relocated here from elsewhere in the vicinity. The old farmhouse buildings have wooden façades, and walls and roofs made from neatly cut slabs of turf. Inside lies a warren of furnished rooms, whose origins range from the mid-1700s to the late 19th century.

At the head of the fjord is **Sauðárkrókur**, the town second only to Akureyri in the area in terms of facilities. From here you can catch a ferry to the uninhabited and rocky island of **Drangey**, which was once a refuge for outlaws. According to *Grettis Saga* this was where Grettir the Strong and his brother Illugi met their untimely ends. The source of the town's hot water is **Reykir**, where the natural hot springs can be visited.

The mountainous **Skagi** peninsula is

Safnasafnið

Svalbarðsströnd
☎ 461 4066
🕘 May-Sep: Mon-Sun: 10am-6pm.
Oct-Apr: closed.
Admission charge.
2 admissions for the price of 1 with voucher on page 69.

Síldarminjasafnið

Roaldsbrakki
Snorragötu 15,
580 Siglufjörður
☎ 467 1604
www.siglo.is/herring
🕘 Jun-Sep: Mon-Sun: 10am-6pm. Shows:
Jul-Aug: Sat-Sun: 3pm.
Oct-May: closed.
Shows: 8 Jul-5 Aug:
Sat: 3pm.
Admission charge.
2 admissions for the price of 1 with voucher on page 69.

Vesturfarasetrið

565 Hofsós
☎ 453 7935
www.krokur.is/~vestur
🕘 10 Jun-10 Sep: Mon-Sun: 11am-6pm. 11 Sep-9 Jun: open by arrangement.
Admission charge.

inhabited less by humans than seabirds, which gather in their thousands on the cliffs of **Króksbjarg** and **Bakkar**. A good vantage point from which to observe the kittiwakes and fulmars is the grassy headland near where the Fossá river plunges into the sea. There are bizarre stepped rock formations at **Vogurviti**.

In the colourful fishing town of **Blönduós** there is a futuristic church (intentionally reminiscent of a volcanic crater) straddling the Blanda river. Salmon fishing is on offer for those with a fat wallet; if not, exploring the island nature reserve is free.

To the south is **Hóp**, a large saltwater lagoon semi-bisected by a finger of land. Separating the lagoon from the sea is **Þingeyrasandur**, a black sand dune created from the ocean's deposits. Breaking up its blackness are clumps of purple thyme, yellow lady's bedstraw and lush lyme grass. Horses frolic in the grass, and seals litter the sand spits at low tide.

The historic site of **Þingeyrar** squats on the eastern flank of Hóp. It was the location for a *þing* (district assembly) and later the site of Iceland's first monastery, now no longer surviving. It was founded in 1112 by Bishop Jón Ögmundarson in thanks to God for restoring the fertility of the land. By the end of the 12th century, Þingeyrar was a centre of learning where monks penned prolific sagas, including that of the bishop himself. A Þingeyrar farmer began the lovely stone church in 1864.

The road around the **Hrútafjördur** fjord to **Brú** passes north of the Vatnsdalur valley and the massive Vatnsdalsfjall ridge. Brú itself consists of little more than a petrol station and a post office.

Hólakrikja

for less

Hólar, Hjaltadalur
☎ 453 6303
🕐 Mon-Sun: 9am-6pm.
Admission charge.
2 admissions for the price of 1 with voucher on page 69.

Byggðasafn Skagfirðinga

for less

Glaumbær
☎ 453 6173
🕐 Jun-Sep: Mon-Sun: 9am-6pm. Oct-May: open by arrangement..
Admission charge.
2 admissions for the price of 1 with voucher on page 71.

Glaumbær

The West

The wind and rain of the west is insufficient to dampen the magic of its historic and literary towns, immortalized in the sagas. This is an area rich in natural splendours, from the majestic Snæfellsjökull glacier (page 45) that can be seen towering over the landscape all the way from the capital, to the caves and craters of Borgarfjörður.

The beauty of the West Fjords (page 45) is wild and savage, a harsh region at the constant mercy of isolation and emigration, storms and avalanches, as well as the ghosts and monsters that populate its vivid cultural heritage.

The cutter outside Byggðasafnið í Görðum

The Ring Road leaving Reykjavík for the north wriggles over the toes of **Mount Esja** before rounding **Hvalfjörður** and descending to Akranes (below). Alternatively, a 7km (4-mile) toll tunnel – Iceland's first – burrows beneath the fjord directly to the west.

However, this short-cut means omitting the hiking possibilities at **Esja**, as well as the two-hour circular walk from the road to the spectacular falls of **Glymur**. Less disappointingly, it also removes the option to detour along Route 36 to the farm where that Icelandic national icon, the writer Halldór Laxness was born. The road also passes the whaling station on the northern shore of the fjord that closed under pressure from international environmental groups in the 1980s.

The belching chimneys of **Akranes** belong to the country's only cement factory. Of more interest to visitors is the extensive **Byggðasafnið í Görðum** (Akranes Folk Museum), opened east of the town in 1959 to chart the district's history. Outside the museum are an 86-ton cutter (1885) and a granite monument donated to the town by the Irish in 1974 in memory of

Mount Esja

Byggðasafnið í Görðum

Garður, Akranes
☎ 431 1255
🕐 May-Aug: Mon-Sun: 10.30am-12noon, 1.30pm-4.30pm. Sep-Apr: Mon-Fri: 1.30pm-4.30pm. Sat-Sun: closed.
Admission charge.
2 admissions for the price of 1 with voucher on page 71.

Borg

Iceland's early 9th-century Irish settlers. The collection of photographs, tools, and knick-knacks indoors recreate a bygone world of country life, from working the land, to minding the hearth and manning the smithy. A special maritime section explores the sometimes fraught relationship between Akranes and the sea.

For those who wish to stretch their legs, it is an easy day's walk to the summit of **Akrafjall**, where it is possible to camp.

The west offers plenty of opportunities to watch birds, such as these puffins

Heimskringla Reykholt

Heimskringla, 320 Reykholt
☎ 435 1490
⏰ Jun–Aug: Mon–Sun: 10am–6pm. Sep–May: open by arrangement. Admission charge.
2 admissions for the price of 1 with voucher on page 71.

The home of Egill Skallagrímsson is commemorated by a sculpture at **Borg**. His 10th-century life and poems were recorded by his descendant the chieftain, legislator, saga writer and historian, Snorri Sturluson (1179-1241) in *Egils Saga*.

Nearby **Reykholt** was Snorri Sturluson's home and the place where he was murdered by his political enemy, Gissur Þorvaldsson. The grisly murder site itself is thought to be the gloomy passage behind the sheltered hot pool. A statue of Snorri now stands in the forecourt of the school here, a present from Norway in return for his writing the *Heimskringla*, a history of the medieval Norwegian kings.

At the **Heimskringla Reykholt** there are displays about Snorri's life and works, including copies of his manuscripts. Apart from the *Heimskringla*, Snorri's most important work is the *Edda*, a source on the old Nordic mythology intended as a guide for aspiring *skalds*, or court poets.

Continuing inland from here towards **Húsafell** reveals an area rich in hot pools,

birch and great views. It is also the
location of three lava caves beneath the
Hallmundarhraun lava field. The largest of
these, at 1.5km (1 mile) long, is
Surtshellir, a former hideout for outlaws.

Returning to Route 54 the road passes by
the **Eldborg** volcanic crater before skirting
the edge of the Snæfellsnes peninsula.
The mountainous centre of the peninsula
separates the sheltered north from the
broader, more exposed southern plain.
This less inhabited southern portion is
reputed to have been the residence of Ari
the Learned, 12th-century author of the
Íslendingabók and the *Landnámabók*.

At the end of the peninsula the
Snæfellsjökull glacier reigns supreme. The
ski runs from the summit in winter are
excellent, and guided walks are on offer
from Ólafsvík in the summer. Attempting
the climb alone is not recommended, as it
is not uncommon for dangerous cracks to
appear suddenly in the ice.

The peninsula's largest town is **Stykkishólmur**,
first settled by the Norwegian Þórólfur
Mostrarskeggi, who named the mountain
to the east **Helgafell**, meaning Holy
Mountain. The mountain was later also
considered holy by Christians. Snorri the
Priest built a church here in the 10th
century in an attempt to secure his place
in heaven.

Even now the mountain is said to possess
the power to fulfil three wishes of all those
who climb it, as long as they conform to
certain rules. The hopeful should ascend
by the southwest without talking or
turning round, the wishes should be made
in good heart and never revealed to
another, and the descent should be made
down the eastern slope.

The sensitively built **Norska Húsið**
(Norwegian House) was brought in pieces
from Norway and reconstructed in 1829
by the wealthy Árni Thorlacius. It is
wonderfully furnished with decorated
chests, paintings and utensils.

Ferries from here to the **West Fjords** stop
at Flatey (page 36) en route. The island's
population has steadily dwindled until now
it is little more than a resort for summer

Snæfellsjökull

Stykkishólmur

Norska Húsið

Hafnargata 5, 340
Stykkishólmur
☎ 438 1640
🕐 Jun-Aug: Mon-Sun:
11am-5pm.
Sep-May: closed.
Admission charge.

Flatey

Látrabjarg

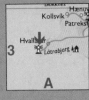

Hrafnseyri

Þingeyri

Sjóminjasafn

Ísafjörður
☎ 456 3293
🕐 Jun & Aug: Mon–Sun:
1pm–5pm. Jul: Mon–Sun:
10am–5pm. Sep & May:
open by arrangement.
Admission charge.

tourists. The mainland route to the fjords
bypasses picturesque villages,
remembered by many Icelanders for their
appearances in the sagas. The action of
the *Laxdæla Saga*, for example, draws on
characters from the settlements
Hjarðarholt, Sælingsdalur and Laugar.

Route 60 traces the wriggling outline of
the West Fjords from **Bjarkalundur** to
Broddanes, the settlements on either side
of this fist of land. The harsh, cold
climate means the western side of the
area is home to very few; this part of the
island has a limited population even by
Icelandic standards.

The twisting road along the southeast of
the fjords similarly encounters little in the
way of habitation. It is worth persevering
to its westernmost point, however, to see
the towering cliffs of **Látrabjarg**, where
puffins gather in their thousands.

The road continues to hug the coast, not
daring to penetrate the interior wasteland
of Gláma. The next diversions are the falls
of **Dynjandi** and the village of **Hrafnseyri**,
where a museum and chapel mark the
birthplace of nationalist Jón Sigurðsson.

Rising to a height of almost 1,000m
(3,280ft), **Kaldbakur** is the tallest mountain
in the West Fjords. The trek to the top is
often accompanied by snow or rain, but the
view makes the effort worthwhile. Nearby
Þingeyri acquired its name from the *þing*,
or ancient assembly, recorded in the *Gísla
Saga*. The Sandfell ridge south of town
can be reached by four-wheel-drive
vehicles or on foot, and the view of the
surrounding mountains is magnificent.

On the other side of Dýrafjörður, between
Mýrar and **Núpur**, is a breeding ground for
eider ducks. The next fjord,
Önundarfjörður, is characterized by a
sandy beach that is crowded with paddlers
when the shallow water heats up.

Ísafjörður is the commercial and transport
centre of the West Fjords, laying claim to
the region's airport and 3,500 of the
steadily diminishing 9,700 inhabitants
found in the West Fjords. The town's
history is covered in the **Sjóminjasafn** (West
Fjords Maritime Museum) in the restored

Turnhús (Tower House). Boats run to the islands of **Vigur** and **Æðey** in the summer.

Separated from Ísafjörður by the Óshlíð mountain is **Bolungarvík**, which similarly graces the southern shore of the Ísafjarðardjúp fjord. There is little diversion here save for small museums.

About 3km (1.8 miles) outside Bolungarvík is an old beaching site for rowing boats, where three buildings are now the **Minjasafn Ósvör** (Ósvör Maritime Museum). One of today's fishermen tells stories of old and demonstrates how the salting house and racks for drying fish were used.

Minjasafn Ósvör

Ósvör
☎ 438 1640
🕐 Jun-Sep: Mon-Sun: 10am-5pm. Oct-May: closed.
Admission charge.

Ísafjörður

On the other side of Ísafjarðardjúp, the torturous road bumps and grinds slowly to **Kaldalón**, a deserted green valley that meets the lower extremities of the Drangajökull ice cap. Beyond here the road peters out at **Snæfjallaströnd**.

The only ways to access the uninhabited law of **Hornstrandir** are by the *Fagranes* boat from Ísafjörður or a long slog by foot. Once there, the only way to explore its pristine wilderness is legpower. The area was abandoned by a handful of desperate farmers in the 1950s, making the way clear for the establishment of a protected nature reserve rich in seabirds, seals, arctic foxes and whales.

Hornvík Bay

The highlight of Hornstrandir is the natural basalt sculptures at **Hornvík Bay**, which most walkers reach from Adalvík via Kálfatindar and Skippaklettur. There is the option of alighting from the ferry at Reykjarfjörður or Furufjörður and walking to Hornvík or Adalvík to catch one back.

Dining

The Humarhúsið seafood restaurant

Enjoying traditional Icelandic cuisine demands an iron stomach and a spirit of adventure. The midwinter feast of *þorrablot*, held each year in February, is one occasion when all the pickled and pungent specialities are served with pride. The main dish is *svið* (cooked sheep's head). The brain, but not the eyes or tongue, is removed, before the head is boiled. The head is then eaten either freshly cooked, or made into *sviðasulta* (head cheese), when the meat is sliced and pressed in aspic with the innards and soured rams' testicles before the whole concoction is pickled in whey.

Other national dishes include *slátur* (slaughter – a sheep's stomach parcel of blood and guts) and *hákarl* (rotten shark). There are two varieties of *slátur*; *lifrarpylsa*, in which the main ingredient is sheep's liver, and *blóðmör* (blood pudding), a much richer dish.

Pungent cubes of *hákarl* are symbolically – and sensibly – taken with generous quantities of that intoxicating Icelandic brew *brennivín*, nicknamed *svarti dauði* (black death). In this way the fumes and fire of the caraway-flavoured schnapps go some way towards masking the putrid stench of a fish that has been buried in the sand for some three months.

Other favourites are salted or smoked *lundi* (puffin), whale blubber, whale steaks and seal meat. A popular snack is *harðfiskur* (wind-dried strips of haddock or cod) eaten with butter. The pristine water and unpolluted environment ensure that the quality of Iceland's fish is unrivalled.

While the fish itself will be familiar to many – *skarkoli* (plaice), *ýsa* (haddock), *skata* (skate), *lúða* (halibut) and the ubiquitous *þorskur* (cod) – the chosen cuts and preparation may not be. Seafood

Perlan

Öskjuhlíð
☎ 562 0200
Restaurant: Sun-Thu: 6pm-11.30pm. Fri-Sat: 6pm-12.30am.
Café: Mon-Sun: 9am-10pm.

Humarhúsið

Amtmannsstíg 1
☎ 561 330
Mon-Sun: 11.30am-11.30pm.

delicacies include cod's cheeks and a number of different varieties of *sild* (pickled herring).

As well as fish, meat and dairy products play a key role in the Icelandic diet. Lamb is a particular speciality, from simple roasts to *hangikjöt* (hung meat) – a filling dish of smoked mutton served with potatoes and peas. The number of delicious cheeses is growing annually, but the one dairy item not to be missed is *skyr* (cream cheese made from curdled milk), eaten as a dessert. This has been enjoyed with cream as *rjómaskyr* for centuries.

Traditional dishes can be found at the Kolaportið flea market (page 13) and in speciality restaurants. One of the best is the revolving Perlan (page 14), with its wonderful (and pricey) views. If it's Vikings that you are after, then the **Fjörukrain** Viking Restaurant is a must. *(Strandgata 5, Hafnarfjördur. ☎ 565 1213. ⏱ Mon-Wed: 6pm-11.30pm. Thu: 12noon-2pm, 6pm-11.30pm. Fri-Sat: 12noon-2pm, 6pm-3am.)*

For the most part, however, Icelandic menus require more appetite than courage. Food is of a high quality and portions are generous. Delicious fresh seafood is served at the **Humarhúsið** (Lobster House). For good snacks, **Café Sólon Íslandus** serves hearty home-made soups with delicious fresh-baked rolls and an olive *tapanade*, as well as large slices of cake with lashings of cream. For a simple yet satisfying Icelandic culinary experience, head to the **Svarta Kaffið**. This small upstairs café with its bird's-eye view of the shoppers below serves beer, coffee and soup that comes in a bread roll bowl.

International dishes are also easy to find, in Reykjavík and Akureyri at least. There are now over 150 restaurants in the capital, including Indian, Chinese, Mexican, Italian and American. An earthy, vegetarian option is **Á Næstu Grösum** *(Laugavegur 20b, entrance from Klapparstígur. ☎ 552 8410, ⏱ Mon-Fri: 11.30am-2pm, 6pm-10pm, Sat: 11.30am-10pm, Sun: 6pm-10pm)*, while excellent pizzas await at **Eldsmiðjan** *(Bragagata 38a. ☎ 562 3838, ⏱ Mon-Sun: 11.30am-11.30pm)*, and tasty home-made pastas and ice creams at **Pasta Basta**.

Café Sólon Íslandus

Bankastræti 7a
☎ 551 2666
⏱ Sun-Thu: 10am-1am.
Fri-Sat: 10am-4am.

Svarta Kaffið

Laugavegur 54
☎ 551 2919
⏱ Mon-Thu: 11.30am-1pm. Fri-Sat: 11.30am-2pm. Sun: 2pm-1am.

Pasta Basta

Klapparstígur 38
☎ 561 3131
⏱ Sun-Thu: 12noon-10.30pm. Fri-Sat: 6pm-11.30pm.

Shopping

The shopping opportunities in Iceland invariably take visitors by surprise, both in choice and quality. What's more, certain items are no longer as expensive as they used to be. In fact, such goods are often sold at as much as 50% cheaper than comparable goods elsewhere – an anomaly explained by shops' low overheads and the need for competitive pricing because consumers exhibit such discerning and expensive taste.

The best shopping opportunities are in Reykjavík, but authentic souvenirs can be found throughout the country, and often at slightly cheaper prices than in the capital's tourist shops. Remember that most shops also offer a VAT rebate, which reduces the price by approximately 15%. It can be reclaimed in cash or on your credit card on leaving the country.

Shopping hours vary enormously throughout Iceland. Most shops in the centre of Reykjavík, however, are open from 9am to 6pm Monday to Thursday, an hour later on Friday, and from 10am to 4pm on Saturday. In winter, some shops open on Sunday afternoons until 5pm. Credit cards and travellers' cheques are widely accepted, and some places offer a discount for those paying with cash.

As to what to buy, the range spans clothes, ceramics and crafts to foods, footwear and folk music. The most popular souvenir is a *lopapeysa*, a traditional handknitted Icelandic jumper made from the soft and naturally water-resistant fleece of the Icelandic sheep. These jumpers were traditionally knitted in natural colours or white and blue. Prices for quality are not cheap, so some prefer to invest in the wool, needles and a pattern and knit their own.

Socks, scarves, hats and gloves are also popular. In Reykjavík check out the range at the **Handprjonasaband Ísland** (Handknitting Association of Iceland). Factory outlets are worth a look, including the very friendly **Íslands Ull** (Iceland Wool).

For international high street shops and

Handprjonasaband Ísland

Skólavörðustígur 19, Reykjavík
☎ 552 1890
🕐 Mon-Fri: 9am-6pm.
Sat: 9am-4pm.
Sun: closed.

Íslands Ull

Þinghólstræti 3
☎ 562 2116
🕐 Mon-Fri: 10am-6pm.
Sat: 10am-4pm.
Sun: closed.

Hans Petersen

Laugavegur 178
☎ 570 7575
🕐 Mon-Fri: 9am-6pm.
Sat: 10am-2pm.
Sun: closed.

designer fashions walk the length of Laugavegur, Reykjavík's "shopping street" in the heart of the old town. A short bus journey north of Hlemmur is the city's largest branch of the **Hans Petersen** photography chain. This has possibly the largest stock of film in Iceland, but the choice is not exhaustive and prices are high.

Other major shopping streets are Hafnarstræti, Austurstræti and Skólavörðustígur, the last of which has exclusive boutiques interspersed with inviting cafés. These include **Eggert** the furrier, which specializes in sealskin coats *(Skólavörðustígur 38, ☎ 551 1121, ⊕ Mon-Fri: 8.30am-6pm. Sat: 10am-2pm).* There is also **Galleri List**, which sells Icelandic art.

Galleri List

Skiholt 5b
☎ 581 4020
⊕ Call for opening times.

A typical souvenir store in Reykjavík

Alternatively, head east of the town centre to the massive **Kringlan** shopping mall, which offers the convenience of 115 shops and services under one roof. These include numerous fashion and food franchises, the gift shop **Íslandia** *(Kringlan, ☎ 568 9960, ⊕ Kringlan hours),* and the well-stocked bookshop **Eymundsson** *(Kringlan, ☎ 533 1130, ⊕ Kringlan hours).*

Iceland's main supermarket chains, **Nóatún** and **Nýkaup**, close at 9pm, while the **Kaupfélag** chain found in the country normally closes at 8pm. Those leaving Iceland via **Keflavík** airport can pick up goodies on their way home, including authentic woollens, illustrated books and typical Icelandic foods.

Kringlan

Kringlan 4-12
☎ 568 9200
⊕ Mon-Thu: 10am-6.30pm. Fri: 10am-7pm. Sat: 10am-6pm. Sun: 1pm-5pm.

Nightlife and Performing Arts

It is certainly true to say that Icelanders know how to have a good time. The energy and effort they put into their working lives is matched by their social excesses. The importance attached to socializing is immediately evident, for example, in the choice and style of the capital's watering holes.

The nightlife has undergone something of a metamorphosis this century. In 1912 all alcohol was banned until 1933, when wine, spirits and beer under 2.2% were legalized. "Proper" beer has been permitted since 1 March 1989, now known as *Bjórdagurinn* (Beer Day). Before this date, the city's massive dance halls were filled with thousands of party-goers consuming copious amounts of vodka and *brennivín* (page 48).

Since then, the popularity of these massive clubs has declined somewhat. Revellers now increasingly frequent the growing number of establishments that have sprung up in Reykjavík's central streets. Fridays and Saturdays are the chosen nights for the *runtur* (extended pub crawls).

Icelanders socialize at home before hitting the bars – a custom fuelled by the prohibitive cost of alcohol (largely due to excessive taxes) and the reliance on potent home-brew to kick-start the evening. All Icelanders buy alcohol at the duty-free shop at Arrivals in Keflavík airport. Visitors may wish to follow their example, as

Uncle Tom's Cabin

Laugavegur 2
☎ 51 1855
🕐 Mon-Thu: 10am-1am.
Fri: 10am-4am. Sat: 11am-4am. Sun: 11am-1am.

Prikið

Bankastræti 12, Reykjavík
☎ 551 336
🕐 Mon-Thu: 7am-1am.
Fri: 7am-4am. Sat: 11am-4am. Sun: 11am-1am.

Kaffi Thomsen

Hafnarstræti 17
☎ 561 5757
🕐 Call for opening hours.

Explosions of lava as seen in the Volcano Show, Reykjavík

alcohol can only be bought at *áfengisbúðar* (state monopoly shops), of which there are four in Reykjavík.

Once the crowds finally make it out on the town, it is invariably quite late, but this is not a problem since most places stay open until 3am. Once the bar stops serving and the lights come back on revellers make their unsteady way onto the streets, or move further down the street to competing establishments that stay open until 5am.

Even mid-week, the same venues stay open until 1am. Equally popular are the trendy coffee bars that have proliferated in Reykjavík and many other towns. These serve beer, coffee and snacks to an endless stream of students and business colleagues, politicians and actors, the sober and the inebriated.

One such coffee bar is **Uncle Tom's Cabin**, an intimate cosy underground café lit with candles, whose atmosphere is conducive to chatting couples and intimate groups. Diagonally across the street is another typical coffee bar, the **Prikið**, meaning "stick". This two-storeyed establishment was named after the bar stools that originally encircled its oval bar. These have since been replaced with more comfortable chairs with arms.

The key streets for raucous evening entertainment, however, are those between the Tjörn and the harbour. On Hafnarstræti is **Kaffi Thomsen**, where carousing customers chat and drink at small round tables against a background of loud music. Opposite is **Astro**, a dancing venue particularly popular with the younger crowd.

Further down the same street is the **Dubliner**, Iceland's only Irish pub. Here Irish music and tourists predominate. This is the place to go for those in need of Guinness, Jameson's or an authentic Irish coffee.

Just around the corner is the large **Kaffi Reykjavík**, where an eclectic mix – from the well-dressed, middle-aged crowd to a more trendy, bohemian bunch – are drawn by its comfy chairs, dance floor and two

Astro

Austurstræti 22
☎ 552 9222
🕐 Fri-Sat: 11pm-3am.

Dubliner

Hafnarstræti 4
☎ 511 3233
🕐 Sun-Thu: 3pm-1am.
Fri-Sat: 3pm-4am.

Kaffi Reykjavík

Bryggjuhúsið/Vesturgata 2
☎ 562 5540
🕐 Sun-Thu: 11am-1am.
Fri-Sat: 11am-4am.

Gaukur á Stöng

Tyggvagata 22
☎ 551 1556
🕐 Sun-Thu: 6pm-1am.
Fri-Sat: 6pm-3am.

Íslanska Óparan

Ingólfsstræti
☎ 551 1475
🕐 Ring for performance details.

Sinfoniuhljomsbvait Íslands

Haskolabio, Hagatorg
☎ 562 2255
www.sinfonia.is
🕐 Ring for performance details.

Þjóðleikhúsíð

Hverfisgata
☎ 561 1200
🕐 Ring for performance details.

bar areas.

Arguably the capital's most buzzing venue, however, is also the country's oldest. **Gaukur á Stöng** offers the winning combination of live music and beer specials every night. The repertoire ranges from up-and-coming local bands to internationally popular artists such as Björk.

Contrary to popularly held opinion, there is alternative entertainment for those unable to face another debauched night on the town, especially in the millennium year. Reykjavík is one of nine European Cities of Culture for the year 2000, with the apt theme "Culture and Nature".

Under the headings Air, Fire, Earth and Water, the interweaving between nature and culture that lies at the basis of Icelandic society is explored and extolled. Throughout the year there is a fantastic cultural spread encompassing every medium, from drama and dance to music and multimedia.

The English-language free publication *What's On in Reykjavík* gives excellent bi-monthly "what, where and when" information. This gives listings for the **Íslanska Óparan** (Icelandic Opera), the **Íslenski Dansflokkurinn** (Icelandic Ballet) *(Listabrout 3, ☎ 567 9188)* and the **Sinfoniuhljomsbvait Íslands** (Icelandic Symphony Orchestra).

Reykjavík's main theatres are the **Þjóðleikhúsíð** (National Theatre) and the **Borgarleikhúsíð** (Reykjavík City Theatre). *(Listabrout, ☎ 568 8000.)* Performances are both international and Icelandic, so even those who don't understand Icelandic are not precluded from finding some good theatre. There is also an excellent theatre at Hafnarfjörður, **Hermóður og Háðvör** *(Vesturgata 11, Hafnarfjörður, ☎ 555 0553)*.

Hugely popular with tourists and volcano enthusiasts is the award-winning **Volcano Show** produced by filmmakers Ósvaldur and Villi Knudsen. The dramatic footage is shown in two parts. The first depicts numerous eruptions, including that of the Vatnajökull Glacier in 1996. The second concentrates on the Heimaey eruption of 1973 and the Surtsey eruption of 1963 (page 26). In the summer there is also an historical filmshow on the nature and people of Iceland.

There are six cinemas in Reykjavík, mostly showing US films with a more limited release of European films. Films are always shown in the original language (which no doubt accounts for the excellent American English spoken in Iceland) with Icelandic subtitles. The cinemas include **Stjörnubíó** (*Laugavegur 94,* ☎ *551 6500,* ⊕ *Mon-Fri: 5pm, 7pm, 9pm, 11pm, Sat-Sun: also at 3pm*), **Bíóborgin** (*Snorrabraut 37,* ☎ *551 1384,* ⊕ *Mon-Fri: 5pm, 7pm, 9pm, 11pm, Sat-Sun: also at 3pm*) and **Kringlubíó** in Kringlan.

Volcano Show

Hellusund 6a
☎ 551 3230, 552 2539
www.centrum.is/
volcanoshow
⊕ Shows: Sep-May: Mon-Sun: 3pm, 8pm. Jun-Aug: Mon-Sun: 10am, 3pm, 8pm.

Golf by the midnight sun

Outside Reykjavík, while the dancing and drinking options may be more limited, there is still plenty to do. From October to March, visitors have a reasonable chance of seeing the spectacular *aurora borealis* (Northern Lights). This shimmering, starry phenomenon of pale green or pink is caused by wisps and streams of charged particles from the sun being drawn towards the earth.

In the height of summer, when daylight lasts for 22 hours, Icelanders acquire a new lease of life, sleeping and working less. Activities that can only be indulged during the short summer months are taken up with a frenzy. Playing golf by the "midnight sun" is as common as it is enjoyable. Akureyri stages the Arctic Open in late June.

Kringlubíó

Kringlan
☎ 588 0800
⊕ Shows: Mon-Fri: 5pm, 7pm, 9pm, 11pm. Sat-Sun: 3pm, 5pm, 7pm, 9pm, 11pm.

Visitor Information

ACTIVITIES

Tours – The range of tours on offer is extensive and exciting. These include luxury sightseeing tours by coach, most famously of the **Golden Circle**. The choice of adventure tours covers ice climbing, kayaking, hiking and mountain climbing. Glacier tours that include a snowmobile jaunt or jeep safari are among the most popular. Specialist bird- or whale-watching tours are available in the summer. If it's wet thrills you're after, consider a white-water rafting experience on the Hvitá, Blandaá or Hjaltadalsá rivers in north central Iceland.

Horse riding – If you are new to horse riding but willing to give it a try, the Icelandic horse is marketed with a good degree of truth as sturdy and gentle. At less than 150cm (59in) high, they are not intimidating as horses go. Lots of companies offer trips lasting from a couple of hours to several weeks. One such is **Adventure Tours** *(Skeifan 18, ☎ 588 9550)*.

Hiking – Walking opportunities in Iceland are unlimited, and with the right clothing even bad weather need not interfere too much. Always inform someone when you go hiking – should you need assistance, you are unlikely to encounter passing walkers. The hiking trails in National Parks and conservation areas are well signposted, but it is wise to have a good map and to talk to locals who will know if certain sections of a trail have become

CURRENCY

The unit of currency is the *króna*, which comes in notes of 100, 500, 1,000 and 5,000. Each *króna* is divided into 100 *aurar*, coins that are of little real value. Banks generally open Monday to Friday 9.15am–4pm, but if you need to change money outside these times most hotels will be happy to help. If you arrive at Keflavík without any Icelandic currency and the airport bank is shut, don't worry as the airport bus accepts all major currencies. Credit cards, Eurocheques and travellers' cheques are widely accepted.

Stables within easy reach of Reykjavík

dangerous after heavy rain or rock falls.

Fishing – Salmon, trout and arctic char can all be fished. For details of private farms and permits, contact the **Angling Club of Reykjavík** *(Háaleitisbraut 68, ☎ 568 6050)*.

Golf – There are now over 25 courses in the country, five of which are 18-hole. For more information, contact the **Golfsamband Islands** *(Icelandic Golf Union, Laugardalur, ☎ 568 6686)*.

Swimming – Swimming is a national institution and geothermally heated pools, many of them outdoor, are found in every community. A stint in a *heiti potturinn* (hotpot) is a must. These warm water pools (up to 44°C / 108°F) often serve as relaxed discussion areas.

A 2-for-1 discount on admission is available for users of this guide to the seven city pools in Reykjavík. The addresses of these are as follows:
Árbæjarlaug *(Fylkisvegur, ☎ 567 3933)*, **Breiðholtslaug** *(Austurberg 5, ☎ 557 5547)*, **Grafarvogslaug** *(Dalhúsum, ☎ 510 4600)*, **Laugardalslaug** *(Laugardal, ☎ 553 4039)*, **Sundhöllin** *(Sundhöllin Barónsstígur, ☎ 551 4059)*, **Vesturbæjarlaug** *(Hofsvallagata, ☎ 551 5004)* and **Kjalarneslaug** *(Klébergi, ☎ 566 6879)*.

Some of the baths offer playing pools, geysers, waterfalls, steambaths, saunas, muscle-tenderizing pots and whirlpools. Contact individual pools for details. All the Reykjavík pools are open from 6.50am to 10.30pm every day.

Skiing – Skiing in Iceland is fairly basic but there are good resorts in both Reykjavík and Akureyri. Nordic skiing can be done just about anywhere in the winter.

Contact the Tourist Information Centre (page 61) to find out more about any of the above activities.

CHILDREN

Children are made to feel very welcome. Those under 12 years of age are eligible for special discounted fares on buses, and quite often at hotels too. Many restaurants offer children's menus and high chairs.

CUSTOMS

Iceland is unaffected by the abolition of duty free within Europe. Passengers have an allowance of 200 cigarettes and 60ml of perfume. In terms of alcohol you may purchase 1l of wine, plus either 1l of spirits, 6l of foreign beer or 8l of Icelandic beer. In addition, you are allowed the equivalent of £145 of souvenirs. There is a duty-free store at Keflavík for both departing and arriving passengers, selling alcohol, souvenirs and books.

DAYLIGHT

From May through to the end of July, it is light practically all day. By contrast, from November to February the hours of daylight are much shorter; it gets light in the south in December by 11.15am and is dark again by 4pm. Often the hours inbetween feel more like dawn and dusk rolled into one, with the sun never really penetrating the grey.

ELECTRIC CURRENT

The voltage is 220 volts, and plugs are the round, two-pin type, so visitors may need an adaptor.

EMERGENCIES

For the police, an ambulance and the fire brigade call ☎ 112. In Reykjavík, call ☎ 525 1000 for an emergency doctor, ☎ 568 1041 for an emergency dentist, and ☎ 1770 for the Heilsuverndastödin (Health Centre) at Smáratorg 1, which is open for treatment outside normal hours. A 24-hour pharmacy is found in the Austurver shopping mall (*Háaleitisbraut 68, Reykjavík,* ☎ *581 2101*).

ETIQUETTE

Visitors very quickly discover that the concept of titles does not apply in Icelandic society – everyone is called simply by their first name according to the old system of patronymics. Very few Icelanders have surnames. Instead, a child takes his father's name and tacks *son* or *dóttir* on the end, to mean son or daughter of. For example, siblings with the same father, Petur, then become Kristjan Petursson and Gudny Petursdóttir.

LOST PROPERTY

Should you lose something while in Iceland, contact the lost and found office (*Borgatun 33,* ☎ *569 9018,* ⏰ *Mon-Fri: 10am-12noon, 2pm-4pm. Sat-Sun: closed*).

Swimming and skating opportunities are easily accessible. If you are in Reykjavík there is skating on the Tjörn in winter, and in the summer children go down to the lake to feed the ducks. Just out of the city centre is the **Fjölskyldu- og Húsdýragarðurinn** (page 17) and the **Árbærsafn** (page 17). The possibilities for keeping children active and amused in Iceland are endless, but great care should be taken if you find yourselves near gorges and glaciers.

CLIMATE

The most important thing to remember about the weather in Iceland is its unpredictability. Generally speaking, south and western Iceland enjoy a relatively mild climate as a result of the warming waters of the Gulf Stream. The downside of this is the accompanying wetness. The further north and east you head, the greater your chances of fine weather, while the interior deserts are notorious for extended windstorms.

The average temperature in the lowlands from May to September is 12-15°C (50-60°F). January is the coldest month, with an average temperature of -1°C (30°F) (temperatures are colder still up in the mountains). Many facilities are wholly or partially closed from September to May.

HEALTH AND SAFETY

Travellers to Iceland should ensure they have adequate health insurance, and check that this covers them for outdoor activities. Iceland does hold reciprocal health-care agreements with certain countries, but it is worth checking if this relates to you prior to your departure.

LANGUAGE

Icelanders are fiercely proud of their language, which has remained largely unchanged since the first Norse settlers. Today it is the only language to still use the old runic symbols ð (ed) and þ (thorn). Protecting existing words and taking care to formulate new Icelandic words instead of adopting foreign words is an issue of nationwide interest. Relatively recent additions to the language have been *þyrla* for helicopter (meaning

The Árbæjarlaug swimming pool in Reykjavík

"whirler"), *sími* for telephone (meaning "thread"), and *friðþjófur* for bleeper, deriving from an old name that translates as "thief of the peace".

It is a very difficult language to master. For foreigners even pronouncing the place names can be a major achievement. Fortunately, most Icelanders speak at least some English and Danish, and sometimes German. As always, however, learning a few stock phrases always goes down well.

Good day	*góðan daginn*
Goodbye	*bless*
Yes	*já*
No	*nei*
Thank you	*takk fyrir*

PACKING

Warm underwear, wind- and waterproof jackets and trousers, hats, gloves and scarves are all essential if you are going to enjoy the elements without catching cold. These items are readily available in Reykjavík, and if you are doing an excursion, the loan of kit may be included in the tour price. Other essential items include a sturdy pair of waterproof walking boots, a blister kit, swimwear (although towels can be hired at most pools), and suncream and sunglasses if you are planning on skiing or skidooing.

Lighter clothing is necessary in the summer. Even in the winter it is worth adopting a policy of layers, as efficient heating in coaches, restaurants and hotels

HOTELS

Accommodation, like everything else in Iceland, can be expensive, but the quality is generally high. Much accommodation outside the cities is not open from September to May, however, and for the rest of the year advance booking is essential. Accommodation options range from international-style hotels to family-run guesthouses, bed and breakfasts, holiday homes, youth hostels and camping grounds. In the more out-of-the-way places, hikers might also choose to stay in basic, self-catering mountain huts. Lists of all types of accommodation are available from the Tourist Information Centre (page 61).

LUGGAGE STORAGE

There is left luggage storage at the BSI Bus Terminal *(Vatnsmyrarvegur 10, Reykjavík.* ⏱ *Mon-Fri: 7.30am-9.30pm. Sat: 7.30am-2.30pm. Sun: 5pm-7pm)*. Many hotels will also store luggage for short periods.

means that you are constantly peeling off and reapplying layers.

The special quality of light in Iceland during the long days of summer, coupled with the spectacular scenery, make photography a key component of many trips. Bring all the equipment (including spare batteries) and film you think you will need, plus a few extra rolls for those inevitable snap-happy moments. In the summer it is possible to use films as slow as 25 ASA, but in the winter and for action shots of whales or horses faster speeds are necessary.

Coaches and cars take a break from the winter roads

MAIL/POST

Póstur og Sími (Post and Telephone) are found in every community. The standard opening hours are 9am-4.30pm. In Reykjavík, the main branch is at Pósthússtræti 5, but there is also a branch in the Kringlan mall. Mail takes about 3-5 days to reach the rest of Europe or North America.

The camera shops in Reykjavík and Akureyri are undoubtedly more expensive and more limited than the stores back home. In the rest of the country, expect to find only standard print, not slide, films. Consider bringing a lightweight tripod (with carrying case) for shooting in low winter light, as well as for evening shots of the "midnight sun" or the northern lights. To warm up "blue" snowy pictures, you could use an amber filter, and to counteract glare and increase contrast a polarizing filter. Make sure you have a proper protective case for your equipment, as the dust prevalent in desert areas can penetrate many Velcro-fastened cases. Plastic bags make a cheap and effective lining for camera bags.

SPECIAL TRAVELLERS

Disabled – Travellers with disabilities will have no problem finding accommodating hotels, restaurants and shops in Iceland, but wheelchair access to natural features is rarer. For advice and the listings booklet *Accessible Reykjavik*, contact **Sfálfsbjörg**, the Association of the Disabled in the Capital Area (*Hátún 12*, ☎ *552 9133*, ◑ *Mon-Fri: 8am-4.15pm. Sat-Sun: closed*).

Students – Although rarely advertised, it is worth asking about discounts. Where specified in this guide, *for less* discounts are available on top of a student discount.

Gay / Lesbian – For information contact the Gay and Lesbian Asssociation, **Samtökin '78** (*Lindargata 49*, ☎ *552 7878*, ◑ *Mon-Fri: 11am-12noon*).

TIPPING

Tipping is not expected; even in taxis you pay only the amount on the meter.

TOURIST INFORMATION

The **Tourist Information Centre** in Reykjavik has a massive amount of information and very helpful staff. There is also a good centre in **Akureyri** (*Hafnarstræti 82*, ☎ *462 7733*, ◑ *Jun-Aug: Mon-Fri: 7.30am-8.30pm. Sat-Sun: 8am-5pm. Sep-May: Mon-Fri: 8.30am-5pm. Sat-Sun: closed*).

TRANSPORT FROM KEFLAVÍK AIRPORT

The most popular entry point into Iceland is Keflavík, from where it is a 50km (31-mile) journey to Reykjavik. The Fly-Bus transfer coach takes passengers from the airport to Hotel Loftleidir, from where you can take bus No. 17 into the town centre or catch a taxi. Buses returning to the airport leave Hotel Loftleidir two hours before flights depart from Keflavík.

TRANSPORT AROUND THE COUNTRY

Between Air Iceland (☎ *570 3000*) and Islandsflug (☎ *570 8090*) most of the country is served by aircraft, which is important when snow makes many roads impassable. Weather allowing, bus is the cheapest way of getting around. For timetable details contact the **BSÍ Bus Terminal** (*Vatnsmyrarvegur 10, Reykjavík,* ☎ *552 2300*). Alternatively, rent a car from **ALP Car Rental** (*Vatnsmyrarvegur 10*, ☎ *551 1570*) or a mountain bike from **BSÍ Travel** (*Vatnsmyrarvegur 10*, ☎ *552 2300*). Bear in mind that the roads can be hazardous.

Tourist Information Centre

Bankastræti 2, Reykjavík
☎ 562 3045
◑ 16 Sep- 14 May:
Mon-Sat: 9am-5pm.
Sun: closed. 15 May-15
Sep: Mon-Sun: 8.30am-
7pm.

CREDITS

Text: Sophie Warne
Photographs: Ed Jackson, Icelandic Tourist Board and Sophie Warne.

Index

Listasafn Íslands

2 admissions for the price of 1 at the **Listasafn Íslands** (National Gallery, page 14)

Valid from March 1, 2000

Stofnun Árna Magnússonar

2 admissions for the price of 1 at the **Stofnun Árna Magnússonar** (Árni Magnússon Institute, page 14)

Valid from March 1, 2000

Norræna Húsið

2 admissions for the price of 1 at the **Norræna Húsið** (Nordic House, page 14)

Valid from March 1, 2000

Kjarvalsstaðir

2 admissions for the price of 1 at the **Kjarvalsstaðir** (Reykjavík Art Museum, page 15)

Valid from March 1, 2000

Hallgrímskirkja

2 admissions for the price of 1 at the **Hallgrímskirkja** (page 15)

Valid from March 1, 2000

Safn Einars Jónssonar

2 admissions for the price of 1 at the **Safn Einars Jónssonar** (Einar Jónsson Museum, page 15)

Valid from March 1, 2000

Listasafn ASÍ

2 admissions for the price of 1 at the **Listasafn ASÍ** (Labour Unions Art Gallery, page 16)

Valid from March 1, 2000

This voucher entitles the holder to the following discount at the **Listasafn Íslands** (page 14):

2-for-1 admission: one free admission with each admission of equal or greater value purchased

This voucher entitles the holder to the following discount at the **Stofnun Árna Magnússonar** (page 14):

2-for-1 admission: one free admission with each admission of equal or greater value purchased

This voucher entitles the holder to the following discount at the **Norræna húsið** (page 14):

2-for-1 admission: one free admission with each admission of equal or greater value purchased

This voucher entitles the holder to the following discount at the **Kjarvalsstaðir** (page 15):

2-for-1 admission: one free admission with each admission of equal or greater value purchased

This voucher entitles the holder to the following discount at the **Hallgrímskirkja** (page 15):

2-for-1 admission: one free admission with each admission of equal or greater value purchased

This voucher entitles the holder to the following discount at the **Safn Einars Jónssonar** (page 15):

2-for-1 admission: one free admission with each admission of equal or greater value purchased

This voucher entitles the holder to the following discount at the **Listasafn ASÍ** (page 16):

2-for-1 admission: one free admission with each admission of equal or greater value purchased

Safn Ásgríms Jónssonar

2 admissions for the price of 1 at the
Safn Ásgríms Jónssonar (Ásgrímur
Jónsson Collection, page 16)

Valid from March 1, 2000

Hið Íslenzka Reðasafn

2 admissions for the price of 1 at the
Hið Íslenzka Reðasafn (Icelandic
Phallological Museum, page 16)

Valid from March 1, 2000

Náttúrufræðistofnun Íslands

2 admissions for the price of 1 at
the **Náttúrufræðistofnun Íslands**
(Natural History Museum, page 16)

Valid from March 1, 2000

Listasafn Sigurjóns Ólafssonar

2 admissions for the price of 1 at
the **Listasafn Sigurjóns Ólafssonar**
(Sigurjon Ólafsson Museum, page 16)

Valid from March 1, 2000

Ásmundarsafn

2 admissions for the price of 1 at the
Ásmundarsafn (Ásmundur Sveinsson
Sculpture Museum, page 17)

Valid from March 1, 2000

Laugardalslaug

2 admissions for the price of 1 at
Laugardalslaug (page 17) **or any of the
seven main city pools** listed on
page 57

Valid from March 1, 2000

Fjölskyldu- og Húsdýragarðurinn

2 admissions for the price of 1 at
the **Fjölskyldu- og Húsdýragarðurinn**
(Family Park and Farm Animal Zoo,
page 17)

Valid from March 1, 2000

This voucher entitles the holder to the following discount at the **Safn Ásgríms Jónssonar** (page 16):

2-for-1 admission: one free admission with each admission of equal or greater value purchased

This voucher entitles the holder to the following discount at the **Hið Íslenzka Reðasafn** (page 16):

2-for-1 admission: one free admission with each admission of equal or greater value purchased

This voucher entitles the holder to the following discount at the **Náttúrufræðistofnun Íslands** (page 16):

2-for-1 admission: one free admission with each admission of equal or greater value purchased

This voucher entitles the holder to the following discount at the **Listasafn Sigurjóns Ólafssonar** (page 16):

2-for-1 admission: one free admission with each admission of equal or greater value purchased

This voucher entitles the holder to the following discount at the **Ásmundarsafn** (page 17):

2-for-1 admission: one free admission with each admission of equal or greater value purchased

This voucher entitles the holder to the following discount at **Laugardalslaug** (page 17) **or any of the seven main city pools** listed on page 57

2-for-1 admission: one free admission with each admission of equal or greater value purchased

This voucher entitles the holder to the following discount at the **Fjölskyldu- og Húsdýragarðurinn** (page 17):

2-for-1 admission: one free admission with each admission of equal or greater value purchased

Árbærsafn

2 admissions for the price of 1 at
the **Árbærsafn** (Árbær Open-Air
Museum, page 17)

Valid from March 1, 2000

Fræðasetrið í Sandgerði

2 admissions for the price of 1 at
the **Fræðasetrið í Sandgerði** (The
Nature Centre, page 18)

Valid from March 1, 2000

Bláa Lonið

2 admissions for the price of 1 at
the **Bláa Lonið**
(Blue Lagoon, page 19)

Valid from March 1, 2000

Sjóminjasafn Íslands

2 admissions for the price of 1 at
the **Sjóminjasafn Íslands**
(Maritime Museum, page 19)

Valid from March 1, 2000

Byggðasafn Hafnarfjarðar

2 admissions for the price of 1 at
the **Byggðasafn Hafnarfjarðar**
(Hafnarfjörður Museum, page 20)

Valid from March 1, 2000

Hafnarborg

2 admissions for the price of 1 at
the **Hafnarborg** (Institute of Culture
and Fine Art, page 20)

Valid from March 1, 2000

Minjasafn Austurlands

2 admissions for the price of 1 at
the **Minjasafn Austurlands** (East
Iceland Heritage Museum, page 31)

Valid from March 1, 2000

68 · Vouchers

This voucher entitles the holder to the following discount at the **Árbærsafn** (page 17):

2-for-1 admission: one free admission with each admission of equal or greater value purchased

This voucher entitles the holder to the following discount at the **Fræðasetrið í Sandgerði** (page 18):

2-for-1 admission: one free admission with each admission of equal or greater value purchased

This voucher entitles the holder to the following discount at the **Bláa Lonið** (page 19):

2-for-1 admission: one free admission with each admission of equal or greater value purchased

This voucher entitles the holder to the following discount at the **Sjóminjasafn Íslands** (page 19):

2-for-1 admission: one free admission with each admission of equal or greater value purchased

This voucher entitles the holder to the following discount at the **Byggðasafn Hafnarfjarðar** (page 20):

2-for-1 admission: one free admission with each admission of equal or greater value purchased

This voucher entitles the holder to the following discount at the **Hafnarborg** (page 20):

2-for-1 admission: one free admission with each admission of equal or greater value purchased

This voucher entitles the holder to the following discount at **Minjasafn Austurlands** (page 31):

2-for-1 admission: one free admission with each admission of equal or greater value purchased

Safnahúsið á Húsavík

2 admissions for the price of 1 at
the **Safnahúsið á Húsavík**
(Folk Museum, page 36)

Valid from March 1, 2000

Byggðasafn á Grenjaðarstaður

2 admissions for the price of 1 at
the **Byggðasafn á Grenjaðarstaður**
(Folk Museum, page 37)

Valid from March 1, 2000

Nonnahús

2 admissions for the price of 1 at
Nonnahús
(Nonni's House, page 39)

Valid from March 1, 2000

Minjasafnið á Akureyri

2 admissions for the price of 1 at
the **Minjasafnið á Akureyri**
(Akureyri Museum, page 39)

Valid from March 1, 2000

Safnasafnið

2 admissions for the price of 1 at
the **Safnasafnið**
(Folk Art Museum, page 40)

Valid from March 1, 2000

Síldarminjasafnid

2 admissions for the price of 1 at the
Síldarminjasafnid
(Herring Era Museum, page 41)

Valid from March 1, 2000

Hólarkrikja

2 admissions for the price of 1 at
Hólarkrikja
(Hólar Cathedral, page 41)

Valid from March 1, 2000

This voucher entitles the holder to the following discount at the **Safnahúsið á Húsavík** (page 36):

2-for-1 admission: one free admission with each admission of equal or greater value purchased

This voucher entitles the holder to the following discount at the **Byggðasafn á Grenjaðarstaður** (page 37):

2-for-1 admission: one free admission with each admission of equal or greater value purchased

This voucher entitles the holder to the following discount at **Nonnahús** (page 39):

2-for-1 admission: one free admission with each admission of equal or greater value purchased

This voucher entitles the holder to the following discount at the **Minjasafnið á Akureyri** (page 39):

2-for-1 admission: one free admission with each admission of equal or greater value purchased

This voucher entitles the holder to the following discount at the **Safnasafnið** (page 40):

2-for-1 admission: one free admission with each admission of equal or greater value purchased

This voucher entitles the holder to the following discount at the **Síldarminjasafnid** (page 41):

2-for-1 admission: one free admission with each admission of equal or greater value purchased

This voucher entitles the holder to the following discount at the **Hólarkrikja** (page 41):

2-for-1 admission: one free admission with each admission of equal or greater value purchased

Byggðasafn Skagfirðinga

2 admissions for the price of 1 at
the **Byggðasafn Skagfirðinga**
(Glaumbær Museum, page 41)

Valid from March 1, 2000

Byggðasafnið í Görðum

2 admissions for the price of 1 at
the **Byggðasafnið í Görðum**
(Akranes Folk Museum, page 43)

Valid from March 1, 2000

Heimskringla Reykholt

2 admissions for the price of 1 at
Heimskringla Reykholt (page 44)

Valid from March 1, 2000

Customer Response Card

We would like to hear your comments about the
Iceland for less Compact Guide so that we can improve it.
Please complete the information below and mail this card.
One card will be picked out at random to win a free holiday.
No stamp is required, either in Iceland or in your own country.

Name: ....

Address: ....

....Tel. No. ....

If you bought the book, where did you buy it from?................

....

If you were given the book, which tour operator gave it
to you? ....

Number of people travelling in your party ....

How many days were you in Iceland? ....

Did you like the guidebook?..

What did you like about it?...

....

Would you recommend it to a friend?...

Would you be more interested in a tour operator's
package if you knew it included the *Iceland for less
Compact Guide*? ....

Any other comments ....

....

....

....

This voucher entitles the holder to the following discount at the **Byggðasafn Skagfirðinga** (page 41):

2-for-1 admission: one free admission with each admission of equal or greater value purchased

This voucher entitles the holder to the following discount at the **Byggðasafnið í Görðum** (page 43):

2-for-1 admission: one free admission with each admission of equal or greater value purchased

This voucher entitles the holder to the following discount at the **Heimskringla Reykholt** (page 44):

2-for-1 admission: one free admission with each admission of equal or greater value purchased

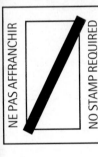

NE PAS AFFRANCHIR

NO STAMP REQUIRED

IBRS/CCRI NUMBER: PHQ-D/2560/W

REPONSE PAYEE
GRANDE-BRETAGNE

Metropolis International (UK) Limited
222 Kensal Road
LONDON, GREAT BRITAIN
W10 5BN

By air mail
Par avion